LifeCaps

The Road to El Dorado

Percy Fawcett and the Lost World of Z

By Fergus Mason

📖BOOKCAPS

BookCaps™ Study Guides

www.bookcaps.com

© 2014. All Rights Reserved.

Cover Image © Zdenko Somorovsky - Fotolia.com

Table of Contents

ABOUT LIFECAPS 4

FAME THROUGHOUT HISTORY 7

CHAPTER 1: IMPOVERISHED ARISTOCRATS 11

CHAPTER 2: INTO THE EMPIRE 16

CHAPTER 3: HOME OF THE EXPLORERS 34

CHAPTER 4: ON HIS MAJESTY'S SECRET SERVICE 38

CHAPTER 5: A TASTE OF ADVENTURE 43

CHAPTER 6: RETURN TO THE JUNGLE 54

CHAPTER 7: FAWCETT AT WAR 78

CHAPTER 8: THE LAST GAMBLE 92

CHAPTER 9: A MYSTERIOUS LEGACY 99

CHAPTER 10: WILL WE EVER KNOW? 104

About LifeCaps

LifeCaps is an imprint of BookCaps™ Study Guides. With each book, a lesser known or sometimes forgotten life is recapped. We publish a wide array of topics (from baseball and music to literature and philosophy), so check our growing catalogue regularly (www.bookcaps.com) to see our newest books.

In 1925, Percy Fawcett left England for Brazil--he would never return.

For his entire life, Fawcett had been fascinated with exploration. The child of an explorer, Fawcett had heard countless wild stories of adventure and it did not surprise anyone that he became an explorer himself.

In 1906, Fawcett made his first expedition to South America; for over 15 years, he made several more. It was in this time that he began formulating the possibility of a lost city.

This book tells the incredibly adventurous life of Fawcett, and what might have happened during this final journey.

Fame Throughout History

People often complain about the modern obsession with celebrities. Sometimes they object to the borderline stalking that goes on just to keep the gossip pages full of topless princesses and drunk actors, and sometimes they object to the celebrities themselves, but either way, the endless fascination with famous people seems to rub a lot of us the wrong way. The current trend towards idolizing those with no talents beyond self-promotion – I mean, what have any of the Kardashians actually *done?* – is certainly annoying, but when it comes to actual celebrities it's not as recent a trend as a lot of people think it is. A traditional name for actors is thespians, and many people think that's the ancient Greek word for "actor". It isn't. It comes from the name of Thespis, a famous actor – Aristotle claimed he was the first of his profession – who was performing in 534 BC.[i] Roman gladiators and charioteers could draw in huge crowds of fans, and some gladiators were paid to endorse products before they fought.

Of course the types of celebrities we follow have changed over time. None of us have ever turned up to watch our favorite gladiator fight, and Aristotle knew nothing about TV personalities (although his opinions on reality shows would probably have made for a good read). But there's one type of person who's been celebrated as far back as records go, and that's the explorer. Whether it was Marco Polo and his voyages to China, or Neil Armstrong landing on the Moon, we're fascinated by the stories of those who push out beyond the known frontiers and bring back stories of new places.

We've mapped and explored almost the entire planet now, and the next great adventure is likely to be the first manned mission to Mars, but less than a hundred years ago it was very different. By the 18th century there were European colonies on every continent except Antarctica, but huge areas remained unexplored. The empire builders were looking for rich farmland and natural resources, and where the land was too harsh or the natives too ferocious they usually just left it alone.

Finally in the mid-19th century, the race to expand empires began to slow. The most ambitious of the European colonizers, Britain, had marked all the land it wanted and either already controlled it or was fighting for possession. France, Belgium and Portugal were snapping up what was left. The one real exception was the USA, where pioneers were setting out to claim the west. After the Revolutionary War and War of 1812 Britain was happy enough to leave the USA alone as long as the USA stayed out of Canada, but in other parts of the world curious British eyes turned towards the jungle and wilderness. There were huge areas within and around the empire that hadn't been explored, and while they didn't have the gold mines or pastures the colonists wanted there were plenty of people who would explore them just because they were there.

Would-be explorers were encouraged by the Royal Geographical Society in London. Established in 1830, this academic society gave support and expertise to planned expeditions and turned the information they brought back into new, more accurate maps and charts. When Charles Darwin set sail on HMS *Beagle* he did so with the Society's support. It encouraged Dr. David Livingstone to search for the source of the Nile, and sent Richard Francis Burton to explore the east coast of Africa. In the 20th century, the Society was involved in expeditions to the South Pole and the summit of Everest. Its support, both financial and technical, gave an expedition a useful edge when it came to facing the challenges of the unknown. That edge often meant the difference between life and death – and sometimes it wasn't enough.

Exploration is a dangerous business, and not all of the Society's pioneers returned to fame and an award ceremony in London. George Hayward was brutally murdered in Afghanistan in 1870. Livingstone was driven mad by malaria and, when tracked down by Henry Stanley's rescue expedition, refused to leave the African interior; he died there in 1871. Robert Falcon Scott, narrowly beaten to the South Pole by a rival expedition, froze to death with his team in 1912. Disease, climate and conflict were ever-present dangers; in addition to the famous heroes like Scott, dozens more Britons died on the Society's expeditions, along with hundreds of native guides and porters.

And some simply vanished.

Chapter 1: Impoverished Aristocrats

Lieutenant Percy Fawcett had never really wanted to join the Army. It just didn't seem like he had any choice.

His father, Captain Edward Boyd Fawcett, was born into a wealthy family in India in 1839. Educated at English boarding schools, he went on to graduate from Cambridge University with an M.A. then joined the British Army as an officer. Highly intelligent and athletically outstanding, he made a name for himself as one of the best fast cricket bowlers of his generation. After playing for the university team he went on to join Sussex County, the oldest of the major English cricket teams. While still young he met and married Myra McDougall, then became a friend of the Prince of Wales. Albert Edward, Queen Victoria's oldest son, was a friendly and good-natured man with a reputation as a playboy. He was also a Cambridge graduate. Before long, Fawcett had been appointed as the prince's equerry, a military attendant to a senior member of the royal family. Officially, an equerry is responsible for arranging the royal's schedule, but for the young Albert Edward that mostly meant organizing parties. Fawcett fitted well into the prince's social circle and did an excellent job as equerry. Unfortunately, he was something of a playboy himself and, unlike Albert Edward, who went on to become King Edward VII, Fawcett didn't know when to stop. By his mid-20s he was well on the way to alcoholism, and his swollen nose had earned him the nickname "Bulb".[ii] Even the fortune he'd inherited from his parents couldn't support his extravagant lifestyle, and by the time the first of the couple's children was born in 1866, the Fawcett wealth was seriously depleted.

The Fawcetts' first son, Edward Douglas, was followed on August 18, 1867 by another boy, whom they christened Percy Harrison. By this time the family had settled in Torbay, Devon, probably for social reasons. Torbay is often known as "the English Riviera" for its mild climate – the Gulf Stream delivers warm water right to its beaches, and it's warm enough year round that palm trees grow there – and the main resort, Torquay, was a favorite of the Prince of Wales. It was also a popular location for the aristocracy – of which Edward Fawcett, despite his falling bank balance, was still a member – to own a summer home. The Fawcetts had another home in Hove, near Brighton, and may have also owned a town house in London – Percy's August birth date would fit with the family being in Torbay for the summer. The location of their own summer home hints at Edward's financial situation, though. It wasn't in Torquay itself but in Teignmouth, a pretty but less fashionable (and cheaper) resort five miles up the coast. Three more children – all girls – were born there over the next 15 years.

Edward Fawcett seemed determined to throw away his entire fortune but his wife Myra was more strong-willed. Perhaps the Teignmouth house was her idea, in an effort to make money available for her children's education. She was determined to send them to the best schools, and somehow managed to scrape up the funds to do it. First Edward junior, then Percy, went off to prep school in nearby Newton Abbot. They then moved on to Westminster, one of England's leading private schools. There's no record of the girls going to school; it's likely that Myra educated them herself, as was common in upper-class families at the time.

By the late 19th century, most of the top English schools had adopted a moral code based on muscular Christianity – lots of team sports, cold baths and evening church services. Westminster was a bit different. It still expected its pupils to meet the social standards expected of the Victorian upper classes, so being immaculately dressed was a necessity, but the school was more tolerant of individuality and outside of school hours students were much less strictly regulated. In fact they were notorious troublemakers in the local bars (there were few restrictions on drinking beer at the time, and it was even common for older students to drink it in school dorms and common rooms). When they were in school they worked hard, both in the classroom and on the sports fields. Percy soon showed he was a natural athlete who had inherited his father's talent for cricket. He was tall and at first glance seemed lanky and awkward, but in fact he was tightly muscled and had outstanding hand to eye coordination. Even as a teenager local newspapers wrote enthusiastically about his skill, but opposing players noticed something else – a grim determination to win that didn't completely fit into Victorian ideas of sportsmanship. A good sport should handle defeat as well as victory, but Percy didn't like the idea of defeat. Either batting or bowling he was a formidable opponent.

Cricket was the summer sport for English schools; in fall and winter they played rugby. The faster-moving ancestor of gridiron football is a world away from cricket but Percy soon mastered that as well, and if anything he was even more of a hard charger. Even the loss of his front teeth in one game didn't stop him from smashing through the defenders to slam the ball down behind their score line. Later he took up boxing; again, his determination was obvious.

When he wasn't playing sports, however, Percy was very different. He was more of a loner than the other boys, and tended to be argumentative. He was also sensitive and found many of the antics of his fellow students appalling. Our puritanical image of the Victorians is exaggerated but Percy really was uncomfortable with what he saw as uncontrollable physical desires, and he developed iron self-control. Constant physical exercise, frequent canings and his struggle to control his emotions combined to create an extremely tough young man. That was just as well.

Percy's father had gone to Cambridge, one of England's two top universities, but that option wasn't going to be available to Percy. Edward Boyd Fawcett caught tuberculosis in 1884, and in September the disease, adding to the damage alcoholism had already done to his body, killed him. After Britain's heavy inheritance tax had been paid there was enough money left to support Myra and her children, but not enough to pay for her two sons to go to an elite university. Edward junior launched himself into a career as an author while Percy, under heavy pressure from his mother, joined the Army.

Chapter 2: Into The Empire

Until the Cardwell Reforms of 1868 most officers in the British Army had bought their commissions. A place as an ensign (equivalent to a US Army lieutenant) in a normal infantry regiment cost £450, or about $137,000 in 2014 dollars. Promotion to lieutenant (US 1st lieutenant) would be another £250, or $77,000. A fashionable unit like the Guards would cost almost three times that. Even after the reforms, when commissions and promotion were awarded on merit and seniority, most officers were expected to have a private income to top up their pay; the cost of uniforms and social events was far more than an officer could afford on what the army paid him. The exception was the technical trades – the Royal Artillery and Royal Engineers.

Even before Cardwell the Engineers and Artillery hadn't used the purchase system, and they also didn't expect officers to have a private income. That made them ideal choices for an upper class teenager whose family was low on funds. There was a different requirement to become an artillery officer, though, and that was to pass the course at the Royal Military Academy in Woolwich, London.

It was even worse than being at school.

Infantry and cavalry officers weren't expected to have any formal military education, because the leadership abilities developed playing team sports at school was believed to be enough – the Duke of Wellington once famously claimed that the Battle of Waterloo had been won on the playing fields of Eton. Engineers, and the gunners Percy was joining, were different. Building bridges or planning artillery fire needed real technical knowledge so the RMA taught its students the basics of chemistry and physics as well as specialist military subjects. Of course, that didn't mean the learning environment there was anything like Percy's father had enjoyed at Cambridge. The course was two years long and cadets in the first year were subjected to harsh, and often sadistic, discipline and hazing by the senior year. At the same time their academic work was punctuated by intensive military training; the infantry might let their officers soak up warlike skills by osmosis, but the artillery and engineers were leaving nothing to chance. By the time Percy Fawcett graduated from RMA in the summer of 1886, his inherently tough personality had been reinforced with military discipline and a carefully developed fearlessness.

The Academy was hard, but for Percy it opened the door to the largest empire the world has ever seen. It's been said the reason the sun never set on the British Empire is that God wouldn't trust the English in the dark, but in the late 1880s it was just the way the world was. A quarter of the planet's land area was ruled from London and the British Army was scattered across that vast area to guard against invasion or local uprisings. That army was surprisingly small for the territory it covered, with less than 300,000 regulars, but it was backed up by locally recruited colonial units. Some of these were very well trained and powerful; the Indian Army was almost as large as the British Army itself and was commanded by British officers. Every garrison had a core of Imperial troops, however, and that meant a young officer could be posted almost anywhere. Percy Fawcett, as an artilleryman, might have ended up in command of a battery of light cannons attached to an infantry brigade or in one of the grim, windswept coastal defense fortresses along the English Channel. Instead, he was ordered to report to 8th Battery, No. 6 (Southern) Division of the Garrison Artillery, in Trincomalee, Ceylon.[iii]

Ceylon, now called Sri Lanka, is an island nation the size of West Virginia that lies just west of India's southern tip. At its narrowest point, the Palk Strait between the island and India is less than 18 miles wide, but Sri Lanka has a long history of independence and a rich cultural tradition. Two millennia ago there was an extensive and advanced system of reservoirs and aqueducts that rivaled ancient Rome's in technology if not size. In fact, in the first century AD, the kingdom of Sri Lanka was a major trading partner of the Roman Empire, shipping spices to Italy through Asia and the Middle East. Sri Lankan dancers were hired to entertain the Caesars – some were witnesses to the assassination of Caligula. By the medieval period it was a wealthy, sophisticated culture marked by elaborate temples and sophisticated agriculture. In the 13th century, however, its power began to decline. Indian warlord Kalinga Magha captured the north of the island in 1215 and set up his own kingdom there, driving the native Singhalese people south and into the mountainous interior.

Portuguese explorers first arrived in 1505, then twelve years later built a fort at Colombo. Over the next decades they slowly took control of the coast, forcing the natives back into the island's interior in a succession of small wars. The Sri Lankans didn't give up, though. In the 1630s, the first Dutch traders reached the island and King Rajasinghe II signed a treaty with them to assist against the Portuguese. Holland and Portugal were at war at the time and the Dutch were more than happy to attack an isolated Portuguese colony, driving them off the island by 1656.

Not long after this more Europeans started to visit – pirates. The buccaneers are normally associated with the Caribbean but in the days of the "Pirate round" from 1693 to 1700, then again from 1719 to 1721, the sea thieves would cross the Atlantic, cruise down the coast of Africa picking off slave ships and traders, round the Cape of Good Hope and break out into the Indian Ocean. There they preyed on pilgrims to Mecca, the treasure ships of the Mughal Empire or, if they felt especially bold, the heavily armed vessels of the British East India Company. Usually they hunted around Madagascar and Réunion, but occasionally they ventured as far as the Indian coast and Sri Lanka. Some even crossed the Pacific to the distant Galápagos Islands.

The treaty between Rajasinghe and the Dutch stated that the Europeans would hand the areas they captured back to the native kingdom but the Dutch, seeing the island as a valuable staging post to their colonies in the Far East, reneged on the deal. For the next 150 years the Sri Lankan kings tried to drive the Dutch out, with no success. Then at the end of the 18th century, back in Europe, the Dutch made a mistake.

Following the American Revolution, the Dutch Republic quickly recognized the USA and began trading openly with it. This annoyed Britain, and a disagreement between the two countries finally flared into a declaration of war in December 1780. The Dutch weren't very worried at first. The American colonists and their French allies had managed to defeat a small British army on land, and the rest of Britain's soldiers were occupied fighting against France and Spain, but they had forgotten that their small empire consisted of colonies that were far from Holland and open to approach from the sea.

Until the 1920s, the Royal Navy was trained and equipped to defeat the next two most powerful navies in the world *at the same time*. In the 18th and 19th centuries, it was at least as dominant as the US Navy is today. Now it was turned loose against the Dutch colonies. The first raids hit Sri Lanka in 1782; Royal Marines captured Trincomalee. They were driven out again by a combined French and Dutch force, but in 1795, with France now a revolutionary republic and the Dutch – minus their royal family, which had fled into exile - their enthusiastic allies, the Royal Navy came back. This time they bombarded the Trincomalee fortress, captured its garrison and took the whole island. Then they discovered that Trincomalee had one of the best natural harbors in the world.

India was the keystone of the British Empire, "the jewel in the crown". The British were constantly wary of threats to it, and now Trincomalee offered the possibility of a naval base that would dominate the Indian Ocean. Prime Minister Pitt called it "the finest and most advantageous bay in the whole of India" and Admiral Nelson was equally impressed. The decision was quickly made; Trincomalee would become a Royal Navy base and Ceylon would join the Empire.

British rule swept away the last remains of the native kingdoms, but it also brought back prosperity to the island. After experiments with coffee growing were ended by a leaf disease the British introduced tea, and soon Ceylon was exporting vast quantities. A local middle class was created and a Legislative Council gave Ceylon a degree of self-government. The naval base remained firmly under Imperial control though, and massive defenses were installed in the old Dutch fortifications that protected it. The gun batteries that lined the thick, low walls of Fort Frederick were manned by the Royal Artillery.

For Fawcett, arriving in Ceylon must have been the defining moment of his life. After a succession of disciplined schools and academies in a land famous for its damp weather, under the grim supervision of his mother, suddenly he was transported to a tropical paradise. He was very junior – a newly commissioned lieutenant – and would have been watched and mentored by his colleagues, but in an Imperial outpost like Ceylon he would have had more responsibility than back home. In England he would have commanded a troop of about forty regulars, experienced NCOs and tough gunners who wouldn't have tolerated much interference from a brand-new officer. Out here, the core of the garrison was much the same but there were also large numbers of colonial troops, ammunition carriers and servants, and in total he would have commanded over a hundred men. More responsibility tended to land on junior officers in the colonies, making it an ideal place to learn his trade.

At the same time it was quiet. The British Empire wasn't exactly at peace, of course; it was so large that it never really was. Troops were fighting the religious zealots of the Mahdi in Sudan along with their Egyptian allies, and a British and Indian force was busy expelling Tibetan invaders from the Indian state of Sikkim. In South Africa, arch-imperialist Cecil Rhodes was hiring mercenaries to overthrow the Ndebele king Lobengula and establish a nation to be named after himself, Rhodesia. Other brushfire wars and police actions sparked and sputtered around the Empire. But none of the enemies involved had a fleet that could threaten Trincomalee, so apart from occasional gunnery exercises, the fortress cannons were silent. As an officer, Fawcett's responsibilities included inspecting his section of the walls, maintaining records of the condition of the guns and ammunition fired, ordering powder and shells to keep stocks up and dealing with disciplinary problems among his men. The NCOs handled most of the day to day work, leaving the young officer with plenty of free time.

No doubt he spent a lot of it playing cricket. Like the Indians, the Sri Lankans took to the imported British game with enthusiasm. The Colombo Cricket Club was formed in 1832; most of its members were British plantation owners or military officers, but dozens of local clubs formed as well and informal games were played in the villages. With his talent for the game it's hard to believe Fawcett didn't spend many afternoons out on the pitch in white flannels and shirt. He didn't spend all his time that way, though. The Sri Lankan landscape and culture fascinated him, and he began spending time exploring. Back in England he would have lived in a small room in the Officer's Mess. Here he had a thatched bungalow to himself, and as well as his personal small pack of fox terriers, he quickly began to fill the bungalow with local artifacts and geological samples.

With its long history of wealth and trade, Ceylon was full of tales of vanished treasure, whether it had supposedly been hidden by defeated kings or buried under a palm tree the way pirates always did in fiction (but almost never in real life). When these stories reached the ears of the British they were usually laughed off; too many people had thrown away time and money looking for legendary gold. Sometimes curiosity was sparked, however. In early 1888, a colonial administrator helped a local headman resolve a problem between two villages, and the grateful chief handed him a note in the elaborate, curving Sinhala script. The administrator had it translated, and wasn't too surprised to find that it told him where valuable treasure was hidden. He'd seen such stories before and didn't give it much credibility, but he'd gotten to know Fawcett over the previous two years and thought the young officer might find it interesting. Fawcett did. Looking through the translation, he read an intriguing tale of gold and uncut jewels, heaped in a cave in the island's interior.

Badulla was an ancient city of the kingdom of Kandy, the capital of a prince who ruled under the authority of the king. Kandy had survived the Portuguese and Dutch colonizations, but finally succumbed to British rule in 1817 after a brief war. By the 1880s, Badulla was a major colonial administrative center and the heart of a prosperous tea-growing area; a rail line had been built to the city to carry the crop down to the coast. Today Badulla has expanded to take in all the level ground in the area, but in 1888 it sat in the center of a flat plain surrounded by wooded peaks. There were many ancient ruins and burial sites, and it seemed as likely a place to find treasure as anywhere. The idea of exploring ancient sites appealed to him for its own sake, but with his less affluent background he had another incentive as well. "As an impecunious Artillery lieutenant the idea of treasure was too attractive to abandon," he wrote to his brother.

The coasts of Ceylon were always bustling with fishing boats and small trading vessels, tiny wooden sailing boats with outriggers for stability. Dozens of them slipped in and out of Trincomalee every day, weaving their way through the towering warships of the Royal Navy. Fawcett hitched a ride on one down the coast to Batticaloa and from there persuaded a cart driver to take him to Badulla.

The note from the village headman seemed promising, but Fawcett soon found out that it wasn't as helpful as it had appeared back in Fort Frederick. According to the directions there was a rocky place at one end of the Badulla plain, and one spot was called Galla-pita-Galla – "Rock upon rock" – by the locals. Under the stacked rocks was a partly concealed cave with its entrance shrouded by the surrounding jungle, and the treasure lay in the cave. Perhaps to explain why the holder of this knowledge hadn't taken the treasure for himself, the letter also warned that the cave was a haunt of leopards, which most hunters think are by far the most dangerous of the big cats.

Of course there wasn't a precise location for the cave, or a sketch to show how it looked from the outside, and Fawcett quickly realized that he'd need to ask for directions. His first stop was a British tea planter. Unfortunately he'd never heard of Galla-pita-Galla; he also pointed out that the plain around Badulla was a bad place to go looking for a specific rock, because "It's all rocks". He did recommend a local chief who might know, a descendant of the old Kandyan kings.

Fawcett tracked down the headman, Jumna Das, and asked him about Galla-pita-Galla. When he explained what he was looking for, Das was happy to talk. He was an imposing figure, tall and erect with an immaculately groomed silvery beard, and Fawcett instinctively trusted him. The message wasn't entirely encouraging, though. Das indicated that Galla-pita-Galla was in the foothills to the south of Badulla, although he didn't know the exact spot, and he confirmed that there were relics of the old civilization around that area. He did caution that there were widespread rumors of treasure. The obvious possibility there was that the letter had been written by someone who'd heard the rumors, and wasn't backed up by any real knowledge. Fawcett looked around the southern foothills and found nothing, so he returned to the coast and back up to Trincomalee.

He hadn't given up, however. He'd taken a month of leave to investigate the story, and it was only a couple of days in each direction. Soon he returned with a group of hired laborers and made a more thorough search for Galla-pita-Galla. Eventually he found a cave he thought matched the description in the story, and he and his men started to dig.

Jumna Das had certainly been right about one thing – there were traces of the old kingdom in the hills. As they dug they excavated fragments of ancient pottery, suggesting that the cave had been used for either storage or as a refuge in wartime. They didn't find a mound of gold and jewels, though.

Finally, through the rhythmic *thunk* of the picks and shovels, they heard an irate hissing noise. Fawcett stepped forward, picking up a lantern. Gliding towards them from the depths of the cave was a white cobra, the front third of its body rearing into the air and its hood spread wide. To Hindus, the cobra is a symbol of the gods Vishnu and Shiva, and is worshipped at the festival of Nag Panchami; white is the color of divinity, making it even luckier. To Fawcett's Buddhist Singhalese workers, however, white was the color of death – and a cobra was just a venomous snake. They scattered in a panic. At that point Fawcett realized it was time to give up. Even if he hadn't found treasure, though, he'd enjoyed the search; he wondered in a letter which a hound enjoyed more, the chase or the kill. He returned to his duties at the fort determined to enjoy the chase at every opportunity.

There was more to garrison life than duty, of course. The social scene was also lively. For the planters, many of whom spent most of their lives in Ceylon, the civil service and military were a source of gossip from Britain and a way to meet potential marriage partners. Fawcett wasn't a naturally sociable man and was wary of the opposite sex, perhaps due to the moral lessons of his schooldays, but more likely influenced by his harsh and domineering mother. He'd written down a fortune teller's prediction in his diary – "Your greatest dangers come through women, who are greatly attracted to you, and to whom you are greatly attracted..." Did he keep it as a joke, or as a warning to himself? Who knows? In any case he was about to put it to the test.

In the spring of 1888, not long after Fawcett returned from his expedition in the hills, the Austro-Hungarian Archduke Franz Ferdinand visited Ceylon. In honor of a minor royal, even if he was from an empire that was increasingly hostile to Britain and its allies, a huge party was organized. It was the social highlight of the year for the local British and the island's military officers, and Fawcett was one of the guests.

Also at the party was George Watson Paterson, a Scottish magistrate working in the south of the island, with his wife and teenage daughter.[iv] Fawcett had no particular interest in talking to a colonial judge, but he certainly noticed his daughter. Unfortunately good manners prevented him from asking her to dance until he had been officially presented to her. After a few discreet questions, he found someone who knew the Patersons and got his introduction.

Her name was Nina and she was seventeen, old enough to be a suitable partner for a 21-year-old officer. Fawcett himself was an imposing sight. Tall and lean – more than six feet tall – he was immaculately turned out in his mess dress uniform. The civilian men were all wearing black tuxedos, and they looked drab alongside the officers. In his tailored midnight blue tunic with red and gold trim, crimson stripes down his pant legs and gleaming leather boots he was naturally eye-catching, and as they were introduced he caught Nina Paterson's – as he planned.

After dancing the two started talking, and if her looks had attracted Fawcett's notice her mind sealed the deal. She wasn't just decorative; she was well educated and highly opinionated, lecturing him about women's rights. Next day he wrote to his mother that he had met the only woman he could ever marry. Soon he was making regular trips to the Patersons' home in Galle. Unfortunately, it was about as far from Trincomalee as it's possible to get in Sri Lanka, almost 200 miles as the crow flies, but he traveled there as often as he could get away from the garrison. Two years later, in October 1890, he proposed. Nina immediately accepted and her family, who had grown fond of the young officer, threw a party to celebrate.[v]

However, back in England, Myra Fawcett was less happy. For whatever reason, she sent a letter to her son telling him that she'd heard Nina Paterson wasn't a virgin. The prudish reputation of the Victorian upper classes has been greatly exaggerated, but this was still a major issue at the time. Horrified, Fawcett broke off the engagement. Nina was devastated by this sudden rejection and left Ceylon to live with relatives in England. Eventually, in 1897, she met and married another Army officer, but he died only five months after the wedding.

Meanwhile Fawcett served out his posting at Trincomalee and was sent on a course at the School of Gunnery in Shoeburyness, Essex. Originally a coastal defense fort protecting the mouth of the Thames Estuary, this was now where gunnery officers went to hone their professional skills. For several months he studied field guns and howitzers, learned how to control their fire on the battlefield and blasted shells out over the wide coastal mudflats. Then he was posted to Falmouth, in Cornwall.[vi]

Falmouth is the deepest natural harbor in Western Europe and the third deepest in the world. As Britain's most southwesterly deep water port, it's a natural gateway to the Atlantic Ocean, and through the 18th and 19th centuries was one of the busiest ports for traffic to North America and the Caribbean; the Royal Mail packet service was based there, for example. That made it strategically important, and in 1539, Henry VIII ordered a fortress built to protect it.[vii] Completed in 1545, Pendennis Castle is located on a headland where it can dominate the entrance to Falmouth Roads and prevent any attacker reaching the harbor itself. Fifty years later, the original fortress was massively enlarged into a huge rectangular platform with bastions jutting from its corners; Henry's castle became an armored control tower commanding far more powerful batteries. Over the centuries Pendennis was neglected several times, as the risk of war receded, but eventually a new enemy would threaten and the fortress would be reactivated and modernized.

In the second half of the 19th century Britain entered a new arms race with its traditional enemy, France, and Pendennis was occupied once more. At the same time naval warfare was changing rapidly as new technology was adopted. For hundreds of years coastal defenses had relied on telescopes and batteries of cannons. However, in 1887, Falmouth was designated as a Defended Port, a militarized harbor that would protect shipping even in a full-scale war, and the fortress was transformed into a state of the art ship killer. Modern breech-loading heavy artillery was installed, along with light quick-firing guns to defend against the new fast torpedo boats. A minefield was laid across the channel entrance, optical rangefinders were installed in the tower, searchlights let the guns fire accurately at night and a telephone network tied the defenses together. By the time the work finally ended in 1943, Pendennis was armed with radar-controlled six-inch gun turrets, but by 1895, it was already a powerful and modern fortress. Before Fawcett went to Ceylon, coastal defense duty had seemed boring; now, even if the scenery was less attractive than the tropical paradise he'd left behind, it was an ideal posting for a promising young officer.

Other things were looking promising, too. Fawcett had found out from a relative that his mother's claims about Nina had been false, and then he heard that she was now a widow. Straight away he wrote her a letter begging for another chance. Nina was reluctant. She believed that his brutal treatment of her in Ceylon had killed any feelings she had for him, but finally she was persuaded to meet him again. When she did, she realized she'd been wrong; her first thought was "We have found each other again". They were married on January 31, 1901, nine days after the long Victorian era came to an end.

1901 also marked another major step forward for Fawcett. His father, before his descent into alcoholism, had been a Fellow of the Royal Geographical Society. Fawcett's own travels in Ceylon now qualified him to apply as well, and he had a taste for more exploration. That year he was elected as a Fellow of the Society, meaning that any future trips he planned would be backed by its formidable resources. His next expedition, however, was initiated and supported by a different source.

Britain had several colonies or dominions in central and southern Africa, but the north of the continent was dominated by rivals – mainly France and Italy, with some Spanish possessions scattered along the Mediterranean coast. Libya and Somalia were controlled by Italy, Algeria and Tunisia by France. Spain had coastal enclaves at Ceuta and Melilla. The one North African country that had managed to resist colonization was Morocco, which had been ruled by the Alaouite dynasty for over 300 years. France was looking greedily at the nation though, both to secure the border of Algeria, and to gain control of the strategic coast. Spain was also interested; part of their reason was that controlling Morocco would weaken the stranglehold imposed on the Mediterranean by the British fortress at Gibraltar. It goes without saying that the British didn't want either of their competitors taking over Morocco unless Britain could make sure there was no threat to its own empire. In 1902, the War Office decided it needed more information on conditions in the kingdom, and started looking for a suitable agent to send. They soon decided on Captain Percy Fawcett.

It seems an odd choice at first glance. Fawcett didn't have any intelligence training and he'd never been to North Africa. He did have some advantages, though. He had a natural interest in other cultures, which had been noted by his commanders in Ceylon. He was fearless, and the mission to Morocco would be potentially dangerous. Finally he was an RGS Fellow. That gave him a legitimate reason to be poking around in North Africa, as well as some valuable specialist knowledge.

Chapter 3: Home Of The Explorers

The Royal Geographical Society's mission was to produce reliable maps of the whole world. Britain was an expansionist trading nation and accurate maps are a formidable weapon if properly used; they can point prospectors towards likely mineral deposits, suggest new trade routes and help armies and fleets manoeuver effectively. Good maps aren't easy to produce, though. Any explorer can come back with descriptions and sketches, and produce a rough map, but it's not likely that distances and positions will be reliable. The RGS wanted perfection. Their idea of a good map was one that would let you, armed with nothing but a compass and the ability to count paces, move from one point to another accurately without looking up from the map. To achieve this they taught their members how to use surveying instruments. A sextant, chronometer and book of tables would let a trained explorer fix their position to within a few yards as long as they could see the sun or one of the main stars. Theodolites allowed angles to be measured very precisely, so by drawing bearings from two known points an explorer could accurately work out the coordinates of everything he could see and the heights of prominent features. The society offered training in these tools to all candidates for membership, and Fawcett enthusiastically accepted. Instructor Edward Reeves was astonished at how quickly he mastered the complicated instruments.

The RGS also gave other training to its members. They instructed Fellows in how to organize and lead an expedition, how to survive in the wilderness and the best ways of collecting mineral and biological samples (including, "where practicable", human skulls). Most of the training was based on a book by Francis Galton, a controversial but brilliant scientist. A half cousin of Charles Darwin, Galton invented the "science" of eugenics but also made important contributions to biology, meteorology and criminology among others. In the 1850s, he had carried out a series of expeditions for the RGS and collected his experiences in the book *Art of Travel*; its advice on equipment ("fish hooks of many sorts… bullet mould, not a heavy one… books to read, say equal to six vols… each man is supposed to carry a long double barrelled rifle of very small bore") and techniques ("A half-drowned man must be put to bed in dry, heated clothes… camels are only fit for a few countries… travelers should always root up the stones and sticks that might interfere with the smoothness of the place where they intend to sleep")[viii] had been gained through hard experience and while a lot of it was already familiar to a professional soldier like Fawcett, it was invaluable to many of his fellow would-be geographers.

The RGS were satisfied that they'd trained Fawcett into an adequate surveyor, but the Army wasn't so sure. For most of the 19th century, artillery had been used as it always had; gunners estimated the range to the target and fired a few shells, then adjusted until they were hitting. Modern guns could fire further than the gunners could see though, or hit targets hidden behind forests or hills. To use them effectively the guns needed to be aimed based on precise map data – another reason Britain was so keen on mapping the world – and the position of the guns themselves needed to be known exactly. Britain's map-making agency is still known as the Ordnance Survey and it used to be part of the Board of Ordnance, which developed, built and supplied all of Britain's military and naval artillery. The Royal Artillery's own surveying course was probably the best in the world at the time and Fawcett was put through that as well.[ix] He learned some more valuable tricks; the RGS assumed that an explorer would be able to visit all the places he intended to map but the gunnery school spent a lot of time teaching students how to accurately fix the location of points behind enemy lines so that fire could be brought down on them. The maps Fawcett made wouldn't just be accurate along his track; he could now plot any point he could see.

Chapter 4: On His Majesty's Secret Service

Despite its huge empire and long list of wars – there are only 22 countries on the planet that it *hasn't* invaded at some point – Britain had no permanent intelligence agency until the Secret Service Bureau was set up in 1909. Before that intelligence was collected by military staff officers, embassy staff, businessmen, merchant seamen – and explorers. It wasn't ideal but there were so many informal agents working around the world that plenty of usable information as collected. The Royal Geographical Society was also a major player in the espionage game. For example, Francis Younghusband became the youngest ever member of the RGS in 1887, aged just 24; in 1919 he was elected as the Society's president. However, Younghusband was also a cavalry lieutenant colonel and frequent secret agent, who played a dangerous cat and mouse game with Russian spies in Turkestan and invaded Tibet with a force of British Indian troops in 1904. He led several spectacular expeditions throughout Asia and definitely deserved his place at the RGS, but he was a dedicated and aggressive agent for British expansionism. Sir George Goldie, who became RGS president in 1905, was a former Royal Engineers officer who outmaneuvered French and German diplomats to bring Nigeria into the British Empire. Now Fawcett found himself being drawn into the game.

In the first years of the 20th century, France and Spain were squabbling over control of Morocco, which was now ruled by the young and ineffective Sultan Abdelaziz. Spain was more of a direct threat to British interests in Gibraltar but France was far more powerful overall. To minimize the threat the British hoped to arrange for Morocco to be split between both powers, with a small – so easily defeated – Spanish enclave facing the fortified Rock across the straits, and a larger French colony inland and to the east. If the two countries came up with a deal London couldn't accept, however, Britain might need to send in troops. If it came to that, they needed to know how to move them around the country. Finding out would be Fawcett's job.

His cover as a geographer on a surveying trip was a convincing one, and gave him an excuse for carrying telescope, binoculars and theodolite. It meant that nobody would be surprised to see him measuring the direction and gradient of roads, and the condition of their surfaces – required information for a good map, but also vital for logistics officers planning to move an army with its supply wagons and artillery. He had a list of other things to find out, too. His diary shows that he'd been briefed by someone referred to only as "James" and ordered to investigate both physical and political questions the War Office needed answered. He noted the locations of villages, their layout and water supplies; did they form natural defensive positions that could block an advancing column, or did they have good wells that would help sustain the army's men and horses? He also observed the local army, noting the strength and location of units, the condition of their weapons and how disciplined the troops looked. His superiors needed to know how much resistance the Moroccans could put up if they decided to fight, whether it was against the British or the French and Spanish.

As well as measuring and observing he also collected "human intelligence" – he spoke to people. Local officials were happy to chat with the imposing English surveyor. He explored the remotest parts of the country, first questioning other travelers then using what he learned to help his own investigations. When he heard that the desert tribes often attacked travelers who strayed off the main routes he disguised himself in traditional robes; with his deep tropical tan, lean build and hawk-nosed face he could pass as a local from a short distance. He scribbled down masses of cryptic notes in his journals, building up a formidably detailed picture of the country and its defenses. Finally he set out to penetrate the Sultan's court itself.

Sultan Abdulaziz was only 23 years old but had already held the throne for seven years. Inexperienced and easily manipulated, he was being influenced by an assortment of European advisors. He was well-meaning and had great ambitions to modernize his country, but he was constantly distracted, and spent a fortune on personal hobbies. Fawcett dismissed him as "weak in character" – probably the most damning conclusion he could have come to – and wrote that he spent most of his time on hobbies including bicycle trick riding, photography, pig sticking and feeding the animals in his private zoo. He didn't have the strength of character needed to fend off the approaches of France, Spain and – most worrying for the British – Germany. Fawcett passed on all his information to "James" and returned to Nina, Pendennis Castle and his guns. Meanwhile, the government processed his reports and decided on its policy. Abdulaziz had been hoping the British would help him resist French influence, so he was appalled when the Entente Cordiale was signed in August 1904. The treaty committed Britain and France to an alliance, and incidentally set Europe on the road that led to the First World War. It also defined spheres of influence in North Africa. As part of the treaty the French recognized British control over Egypt; in return, Britain gave up any interest in Morocco, giving the French a free hand to occupy it. Within three years, Abdulaziz had been overthrown, and by 1912, Morocco had been split into French and Spanish protectorates – with, as Britain had planned all along, the Spanish facing Gibraltar.

His trip to Morocco was the only one Fawcett ever made working purely as an agent, but his thorough work and ingenuity were noticed. From now on, when the British government wanted a skilled observer for a job, his name would be on the list.

Chapter 5: A Taste Of Adventure

After returning from Morocco Fawcett was posted again, with a brief stay in Hong Kong then a return to Trincomalee in late 1902.[x] This time he was accompanied by Nina, who must have been just as pleased as he was to be returning to the island. Nina was pregnant with their first child when they made the long voyage round South Africa and across the Indian Ocean, and she was delighted that she would be giving birth in the tropical paradise where she had been born herself.

Jack Fawcett was born on May 19, 1903 in Trincomalee. The date was a significant one in the Buddhist calendar; the moon was half full that night, and the half-moon in May (or the first half-moon if there are two of them) is the Ploughing Festival which commemorates Buddha's first moment of enlightenment. Fawcett's older brother Edward had adopted Buddhism during a visit to Ceylon in 1890 and Fawcett had developed an interest in the subject himself. According to letters he wrote to Nina over the next several years, the coincidence of the date had convinced him Jack had been born to carry out some great purpose. At the same time, Fawcett himself was looking for the purpose in his own life, and was starting to suspect it wasn't going to be found in an endless series of postings to garrisons throughout the empire.

Bored, he set out from the fortress one day and ploughed his way through the thick jungle in search of adventure. He'd been told that, in and around the modern city of Anuradhapura, there was another city – an ancient ruined one, slowly disintegrating as roots and vines pried its stones apart. He knew the rough location but still the journey and the search took him hours. Finally he found what he was looking for. Surrounded by Buddhist monasteries, the sacred city coexisted with the rubble of an ancient capital. The first thing he found was a wall, half-buried in the debris of the jungle floor. He scraped away some moss from the weathered stone, revealing intricate carvings of elephants – dozens of them. Moving out from the wall in an expanding spiral he soon came across more ruins; the remains of temples, homes and the palaces built when this isolated place was the capital of first-century Ceylon. For hours he poked around among the relics, stopping occasionally to sit on a stone and look around in awe as he sipped warm water from his felt-covered canteen. This, he decided, was what he wanted to do with his life – exploring.

The Army, as it often does, had other ideas. Despite the growing demands for home rule, or even independence, Ireland was still part of the United Kingdom at the time and its ports were an important link in the Atlantic shipping routes. It was also a forward base for the Royal Navy's forces tasked to operating in the Atlantic, and their main base on the south coast of Ireland was Cork Harbour. In late 1903, Fawcett, now promoted to Major, was posted to the garrison there.

Like Falmouth, Cork was defended by a fort armed with heavy artillery, this one located on Spike Island in the mouth of the harbor. From above Fort Westmoreland looked like a flattened hexagon, with bastions projecting from each corner so any attempt to attack it could be shredded by cannons firing in from the flanks. It had been built in the 1780s, when fortification had become a science, and each angle had been carefully calculated so that every inch of the walls could be swept by the guns in at least one bastion. Each bastion in turn had flank batteries that could fire straight along the faces of its neighbors; no attacker could approach Fort Westmorland without being caught in a tangled storm of gunfire coming in from at least two directions. Now the Royal Artillery was making it even more formidable, with modern six-inch guns and searchlights to blast attacking ships and machine guns and quick-firers for close in defense. Again like Falmouth, it was an important fortress, but this time Fawcett was less interested. Ireland is a famously damp place, and under the drizzling gray sky he was constantly dreaming of jungle adventures. When the Royal Geographical Society asked him to mount a new expedition for them, he agreed immediately.

Fawcett had been in Ireland for just over two years, and he was desperate for a real challenge. There was occasional trouble in Ireland but it was directed against the police and small military patrols; the rebels weren't going to challenge Fort Westmorland's garrison, and Fawcett had no urge to turn his massive guns on Irish civilians. Now, in early 1906, he was being offered an adventure. As quickly as he could get permission from his commanding officer he took a boat to the mainland and made his way to the RGS in London.

Today, 1 Savile Row is the home of upmarket tailor Gieves & Hawkes. Their predecessor, Hawkes & Co., had supplied clothes to many explorers; in 1912, the grateful RGS, about to move to a larger headquarters, sold them the old four-story corner house for the bargain price of £38,000. When Fawcett arrived there in early 1906 it was still very much the home of the Society, ruled by the fiery Sir George Taubman Goldie. Now the 33-year-old was shown into the great man's office. Straight away Goldie asked, "Do you know anything about Bolivia?"[xi]

Fawcett didn't, but then nor did anyone else – even, as it turned out, the Bolivians. Goldie spread a map on his desk, explaining that it was the best one available. The west of the country was quite well mapped, he pointed out, but to the east was a vast area of tropical forest and plains. Most of it was a mystery. Bolivia bordered Peru to the northwest and Brazil to the north and east, but the borders themselves were hotly disputed and nobody knew exactly where they should be on the ground. For a long time it hadn't mattered because it was just uninhabited wilderness, but now it was important.

As the market for consumer goods grew in Europe and North America, so did the demand for rubber. Huge plantations were being carved out of the South American jungle and the land was suddenly a valuable asset. There had already been a murderously destructive war between Paraguay on one side and Brazil, Uruguay and Argentina on the other, which had killed well over half the Paraguayan population. Now growing tension between Brazil and Bolivia threatened more bloodshed. Looking across the border at Paraguay, where about 220,000 people survived from a nation that had once numbered close to 900,000, they were keen to avoid war if possible. The solution they settled on was to ask a neutral third party to survey the area and decide on the borders, and they chose the Royal Geographical Society.

The RGS was an ideal choice; Britain didn't have any colonies or close allies in South America, and was powerful enough to resist pressure from anyone else in the region. The Society's geographers were also highly trained and respected around the world, so Brazil and Bolivia could rely on them to do a good job. It was a potentially dangerous mission though; the terrain was incredibly harsh, and the native Indians were often hostile. Goldie wanted someone tough and resourceful for the job, and Fawcett seemed ideal. Of course, he's also shown that he was a skilled observer, and while Britain didn't have any direct interests in the area, it was always good to find out as much as possible about what was happening in the world. By sending Fawcett to carry out the survey, the RGS could make sure that Britain knew as much about the new border and the land on either side of it as Brazil and Bolivia did.

The plan was for Fawcett to hire most of his team when he arrived in Bolivia, but he couldn't be the only RGS representative in the party; that would mean that if anything happened to Fawcett – and, as he was soon to find out, something easily could – the expedition would be a failure. His companion for this trip would be Arthur John Chivers, an engineer and surveyor.

The two sailed to the USA, then down the coast to Panama where they caught a train south. Finally they reached the Bolivian capital, La Paz. For the first time Fawcett ran into the mess that was South American bureaucracy, as he waited for the Bolivian government to release the funding they had agreed to give the expedition. When they finally did – it took a month – it was a lot less than Fawcett had been told to expect back at the RGS. His decisive personality caused clashes with the local officials and the British consul had to step in to resolve the dispute, but eventually he managed to get enough money to buy pack animals and cover the cost of the expedition. He also had a copy of the unofficial RGS handbook *Hints to Travellers* and his diary, in which he'd written down some of his favorite poems.

The first stage was to cross the Andes and reach the Amazon basin where the survey would be carried out. The two men led their mules through the high mountain passes, sometimes gasping in the freezing, thin air 20,000 feet up. Once across the ridge, they descended into increasing humidity until they reached the lawless rubber towns along the edge of the forest. There was immense wealth sloshing around here, but it was beyond the reach of civilization, and the rubber companies treated the locals appallingly. A British inquiry later estimated that one company had worked over 30,000 immigrants and local Indians to death. Laden with valuable equipment, the two explorers were extremely wary. Slavery was rife, they discovered. Company thugs routinely wiped out Indian villages. Fawcett quickly developed an intense loathing of the rubber companies, and publicly described their slave masters as "scum" and "savages".

49

In early September 1906, the pair was in the town of Riberalta, deep in the Amazon and close to the disputed border. They hired the rest of their party here; it was a wild, rough place, but they stood a good chance of finding men who could survive in the jungle. In the end they selected twenty men, a mix of fortune hunters and native scouts. The two best were Willis, a Jamaican prospector with a gift for foraging and cooking, and a former Bolivian army officer who spoke fluent English and could translate for them. They made their final preparations before striking out into the jungle, and Fawcett gave the men a lecture about how he planned to run the expedition. His words rammed home the point about the dangers they would face.

Most importantly, he pointed out, the party had no way of carrying a sick or seriously injured man along with them. If they tried it would slow them down so much that they would run out of food before they could escape from the jungle. The solution was simple; anyone who broke a leg or caught a crippling fever would face a stark choice. They could commit suicide with an overdose of opium pills, or be left to face starvation while the rest carried on. It was brutal, but necessary; in the days before radios and rescue helicopters there was no alternative. Anyone who couldn't stay with the group was on their own.

On September 25 everything was as ready as they could make it, and the group set off from Riberalta into the unmapped depths of the Amazon rainforest. They had a heavy load of equipment and their planned route through the disputed area was nearly 600 miles long, so they couldn't carry everything on their backs, but it would be impossible to take pack animals through the dense jungle. Instead they bought dugout canoes in Riberalta and set off down the river that flowed through the town, the Madre de Dios. The Amazon basin is criss-crossed with rivers, most of them tributaries of the Amazon itself, and travel by boat would take them to within a few miles of anywhere they wanted to go. That didn't mean it would be easy though. The rivers were alive with hazards. Piranhas aren't the rapacious pack hunters many people believe, but they can still deliver a nasty bite. Electric eels can instantly stun a man with a 600-volt shock, leaving him helpless and drowning. The green anaconda, the world's heaviest snake, is mostly aquatic and has been known to occasionally attack and eat humans. The water is also infested with leeches and the small but alarming candiru catfish, and the currents and obstructions of the river itself can be lethal to anyone in a small boat. They found that the channels were often blocked by fallen trees that they had to hack through with axes and machetes. And then there were the Indians.

After the way they were treated by the rubber companies it's not surprising the Indians could be hostile. Some of the tribes had fearsome reputations of their own, and Fawcett had thought about how to deal with them. In the end he decided to be as non-aggressive as possible, and only use guns to defend themselves as a last resort. Travelers who knew the area told him this plan was suicidal, but in the end Fawcett was proved right. His expedition all carried rifles for hunting and revolvers for self-defense, but the Indians with their blowpipes and bows would have been able to pick them off from ambush.

There were still confrontations with the Indians, one of them ending in tragedy. A river pilot they'd picked up scouted ahead to find a way around a series of rapids, and never returned; Fawcett led a search party to find him and discovered his body, riddled with dozens of arrows. Another time Indians shot at them from the bank, and Fawcett observed that the longbows they were using were lethally powerful; one arrow smashed through the inch and a half thick wood of his canoe. But their worst enemies were far smaller and more insidious – mosquitoes.

Mosquitoes are a pest in every damp tropical region, and the Amazon was infested with them. Female mosquitoes, notoriously, are bloodsuckers; their bites cause a maddening itch. More seriously they can transmit a whole range of diseases, and in South America the most serious are malaria and yellow fever. Yellow fever is normally a mild disease that passes quickly, but one victim in seven will develop a more severe form and a fifth to half of those will die. Malaria is a disabling disease at best but can also cause encephalitis, often resulting in coma and death, or the terrifying and lethal complication known as blackwater fever. As the weeks passed more and more of the men fell sick, and the unlucky ones started to die. At one point, four of Fawcett's crew died in a matter of days and were buried beside the river. But the survivors pressed on.

Fawcett was pushing them hard. Some of the men on this and later expeditions thought he was a tyrant, but there was a lot of sense in his methods. He knew that the longer they were in the jungle, the more they would succumb to disease, and he wanted to explore and map the border area as fast as possible. As they went he experimented with different ways of keeping the insects off – sealing the palm-leaf roofs of the boats with mosquito netting, or sleeping in the smoke from their camp fires. Nothing worked. Even the nets they draped over their hammocks were little protection, as tiny biting gnats crawled in through the mesh. Miniscule bees drank their sweat and the moisture from their eyes, and termites chewed their clothing and rucksacks. Chivers caught fever, and became so ill that Fawcett sent him and a group of the other men back to Riberalta. Two of them died of fever before they got there. The expedition shrank further. Finally only Willis, the interpreter, and Fawcett himself were left.

Now Fawcett learned something important – a small group of fit men could move much faster than a larger party. The three of them pressed on, plotting the course of the border along the Rio Guapore then striking out overland. In May 1907, eight months after the expedition had set off, they emerged from the jungle with their precious map of the border region.

First the Bolivian/Brazilian boundary commission, then the RGS, were astonished when Fawcett delivered his map. The survey had been expected to take eighteen months, and he'd done it in less than half that. It was the start of his reputation as an Amazon explorer.

Chapter 6: Return To The Jungle

Within months of his triumphant return from the rainforest, and after a short visit to England to see his family – his second son, Brian, had been born while he was mapping the border - Fawcett was back in Bolivia and preparing to set off again. He had a new deputy this time, Frank Fisher. Fisher, who like Chivers – now recovering in hospital – was both an engineer and an RGS member, wasn't completely sure about Fawcett's new plan. The RGS contract with the boundary commission only covered mapping the border but now Fawcett wanted to explore the Rio Verde, a small tributary of the Rio Guapore, and trace it back to where it began. There was nothing wrong with the idea, but there was no real need to do it either and Fawcett had barely recovered from the insect bites and malnutrition he'd suffered on the first expedition. It seems he'd already been captured by the thrill of exploring; he was going to find the source of the Rio Verde just because he could.

Tourists now ride the rapids of the Rio Verde in truck inner tubes, and there are adventure trails through the forest where people roam to watch birds and monkeys playing in the trees. Modern insect repellant and some careful drainage keep the mosquitoes to a manageable level. It was different in 1907. Once you ventured north of Corumbá, the expedition's starting point, the region was virtually unexplored. The Indian tribes were wary and hostile, and the river itself was fast-flowing and dangerous. Still, Fawcett was determined to both map the course of the Guapore and find its source. Once Fisher had agreed to come with him he started looking around for reliable companions, this time aiming to keep the team as small as possible. In the end, he settled for seven more men. He was gambling with their safety, he knew. His policy of non-violence towards the Indians was, in his own words, a "mad risk", and with such a small group there would be little they could do to fight off an Indian ambush anyway. Still, he thought it was worth it. Weighing up the dangers they would face, he had come to the conclusion that while Indians might kill them, if they spent long enough out there the jungle definitely would. A small team could move faster, and complete the trip before death became inevitable.

From Corumbá they struck out north on foot, carrying their supplies on mules. This first leg of the journey took them along 400 miles of jungle tracks before they reached the river. Then they built two rafts from balsa logs, turned the mules loose to fend for themselves and began fighting their way upstream.

Many of the rivers in the Amazon basin are broad and deep, flowing placidly between heavily wooded banks. This stretch of the Guapore was more treacherous, with frequent rapids. At every obstruction or bend in the river Fawcett would take a sight with his sextant to confirm its location, and use compass and theodolite to record the height and bearings of the surrounding hills. Slowly the almost-blank map began to fill in with precious details. It was hard work though. Often, to get clear of the jungle canopy to use his instruments, Fawcett had to find high ground then climb to the top. These forays exposed him to the danger of attack by animals or Indians, but they were essential if he was to draw an accurate map. Other times they had to unload the rafts and drag them along the river bank beside rapids too dangerous to pass by water.

Finally they came to a series of rapids flanked by steep ground they couldn't haul the rafts over. There were only two options open. One was to give up and head back down the river the way they'd come. Fawcett chose the other. He ordered the men to strip their kit to the bare essentials – rifles, machetes, water bottles, hammocks and surveying instruments – and prepare to continue on foot. Any spare corners of their rucksacks were crammed with rations, but they only had enough food for a few days. Soon they would be forced to live off what they could find in the jungle.

The terrain was awful. Deep under the canopy the rainforest is a surprisingly sterile place. Not much sunlight penetrates the leaves, so the floor is bare apart from the huge columns of the trees themselves. Anything that falls to the floor – branches, leaves, dead animals – is quickly consumed by ants and beetles. If a tree falls and rips a bright gap in the forest there's an explosion of growth as saplings race upwards, but finally one wins and the hole in the canopy is sealed again; the slower trees weaken in the gloom, die and are eaten. Along rivers, however, sunlight can slant in for hundreds of yards through the trunks. The result is a nightmare tangle of thick undergrowth, bamboo and low scrubby trees. That was what the expedition, tied to the river they were following, had to fight through. At every step they were confronted by a dense wall of green; the only way forward was to hack a path. Arms ached with the effort of swinging the machetes they gripped in blistered, bleeding hands. The muddy soil clumped on their boots, making each step a dragging effort. The sweat-sucking bees whined maddeningly around their heads. Even rising before dawn and slashing forward until nightfall, with only short breaks for water or a hasty meal, their progress was grindingly slow. Often they were lucky to make fifty yards in an hour, and their nightly camps were rarely more than half a mile apart. Still, Fawcett and Fisher used their sextants to pinpoint every feature, and the map slowly filled in.

Things weren't going well, though. They'd been short of food from the moment they abandoned the rafts, and Fawcett had relied on the men's discipline to make what they had hold out as long as possible. It didn't work. Most of them failed to ration themselves and ate their entire supplies in the first couple of days. By the ninth day after setting out on foot there was nothing left. Hoping to hunt and forage, Fawcett led them away from the river bank and into the dark cathedral-like space under the canopy. To his horror, he found it was almost bare of life. In fact, there were animals all around, but in this fiercely competitive environment they had evolved into masters of concealment. The creatures of the rainforest heard them coming and hid. Even the river, when they fought their way back to it, let them down. There were no fish. Tannic acid, produced naturally in the bark of tropical hardwoods, leached into the water from decaying trees and killed the tiny crustaceans that young fish fed on.[xii] Nothing lived in the Rio Verde except plankton.

For a month they pushed on through the forest, living on palm cabbage – the soft young leaf shoots from the center of a palm tree's foliage – and an occasional handful of nuts. Fisher was gripped by an uncontrollable fever. Another man was crippled by a falling branch; he could limp just fast enough to keep up but the others had to split his load. They kept going, growing weaker as they went. Finally they reached the headwaters of the river. Fawcett dragged himself up another slope to point his sextant at the sun, then triumphantly marked the location on the map. Now all they had to do was get out of what the men had nicknamed the Green Hell.

They were all very weak now; a photo taken by Fawcett at the head of the river shows a group of thin, hollow-faced phantoms.[xiii] The journey home would be mostly downhill, so they shouldn't need so much energy, but it was vital to get clear of the jungle as fast as possible. Unfortunately, it wasn't as easy as that. The terrain was sandstone, sedimentary rock, and over millions of years the interlaced rivers had carved away huge chunks of it to leave towering cliffs. Time and again they found themselves standing at the top of a precipice. If they'd been fresh they might have managed to climb down the rock but now, feeble from starvation, they just didn't have the strength. All they could do was back off and look for another path. More weeks passed, and they grew even weaker. Their bodies stripped away their last reserves of fat then began breaking down muscles. Metabolisms slowed in a desperate attempt to save energy, making it harder to get the men on their feet every morning. One man collapsed and refused to get up until Fawcett unsheathed his hunting knife. It couldn't last though. A few days later they were all on the edge of passing out, stumbling onwards in a trancelike state. If anyone collapsed now the others probably wouldn't even notice; they'd just keep going until one by one their own strength ran out. Then, just before the end, Fawcett saw a deer.

The rifle weighed nine pounds and he had barely enough strength left to raise the butt to his shoulder. As the barrel came up the muzzle wavered in wild circles. Focusing all his strength on the distant animal he slowly managed to settle the sights on it, held his breath and fired. The deer bounded off into the jungle – then dropped.

Grilled over a fire and its bones quickly gnawed clean, the deer gave them enough energy to press on towards the edge of the jungle. Five days after shooting it they reached a settlement. It was a *Quilombo*, a jungle village set up by escaped African slaves.[xiv] Slavery was finally abolished in Brazil in 1888 but many of the villages survived, and they had a tradition of taking care of fugitives. Fawcett and his men were in good hands. Unfortunately, it was too late for most of them. Hideously weakened by starvation, five died shortly after they reached the *Quilombo*. Only Fawcett, Fisher and two others finally made it out of the jungle, and they had all learned valuable lessons.

Fawcett was determined to learn more. He returned to Bolivia in 1909 and mapped another stretch of the border. He also spent time talking to the Indians every chance he got. Sometimes he was treated with suspicion and hostility, but gradually some of the tribes started to thaw as his non-aggressive approach won their trust. He learned how to call deer and other animals with a whistle, and how to use bird lime – sticky sap – to catch birds as they landed on a branch. The Indians taught him to find brazil nuts and other edible plants in the jungle, and how to add the sap of *Euphorbia cotinifolia* – the smoke bush – to a pool or slow-moving stream, where the narcotics it contained would stun the fish and bring them to the surface. By the time he returned to England again he was far more at home in the jungle and felt confident he would never again face starvation as he had the year before.

Around this time Fawcett made an interesting connection through his brother's spiritualist circles. Sherlock Holmes author Sir Arthur Conan Doyle had perfected many of the deductive techniques that his fictional detective used, but was also deeply interested in spiritualism and the occult; he was famously fooled by the Cottingley Fairies, images produced by two young girls with a primitive camera and a talent for drawing. Conan Doyle was often around the fringes of the groups Edward Fawcett was involved with, and now he met Fawcett himself. He listened for hours to the explorer's tales of the jungle and the rumors of ancient secrets it contained. As Fawcett's fame spread the author decided to write a novel set in the same region, and the result was *The Lost World*. Published in 1912 it told of an isolated Jurassic wilderness, high on one of the limestone plateaus Fawcett had told him of, where dinosaurs and primitive men survived. The hero, Professor Challenger, went on to feature in two more novels and several short stories. Unlike the calm, scientific Holmes he was an energetic, impetuous and often short-tempered man – very much like Fawcett.

As Conan Doyle was sketching the outlines of his novel, Fawcett himself was preparing to return to the jungle. His next task was to solve yet another border dispute, this time between Bolivia and Peru. The boundary between the two countries runs close to the Heath River and Fawcett was asked to set a line both countries could agree on.

This time he decided to recruit the core of his expedition in England instead of relying entirely on locals, so he put advertisements in several newspapers asking for volunteers. He was no longer an unknown army officer – his first expeditions had been reported in the British press – and there wasn't any shortage of volunteers. That let him be selective. Most of the responses were rejected right away, and after interviewing the rest he picked six to go with him. One of them was a young doctor named Simpson. Another was 26-year-old Henry Manley, a wannabe explorer who hadn't had the money or connections to launch his own expedition yet. The rest were all former soldiers; they included ex-Corporal Todd, who'd served with him in the Royal Artillery,[1] Sergeant Leigh and former Lieutenant Gibbs. Then there was Henry Costin. Another former corporal, Costin was a veteran of the elite Rifle Brigade[xv] (as was Leigh) who'd become bored with army life. Awesomely fit, he'd been a physical training instructor and had competed in the Army's covered Bisley marksmanship contest. Short, tough, powerfully built and with an extravagant mustache, he could have come straight off the cover of one of the adventure novels that were becoming popular at the time. For Costin, patrolling the borders of the largest empire the world had ever seen and fighting endless colonial wars had become dull; as soon as he saw Fawcett's ad he jumped at the opportunity. Along with Manley, the indestructible little infantryman would become Fawcett's most reliable companion.

---

[1] In 1920 the rank of Corporal in the Royal Artillery and Royal Horse Artillery was replaced by Bombardier.

Costin, Leigh, Manley and Todd traveled to Bolivia with Fawcett; Simpson and Gibbs joined them later in La Paz. They also signed on two young Bolivian officers and, later, an employee of the Inca Rubber Company. Tales of the region's wild Indians frightened the new additions, though. The rubber buyer deserted the first time he saw the prints of bare feet on the path, and one of the Bolivian officers developed an illness that Fawcett found suspiciously convenient and was left behind at a town on the Madre de Dios River. Fawcett also wanted to take three Bolivian soldiers to help carry the equipment but he quickly found they couldn't be trusted to stick to their allowed food ration, and sent them back. That left seven men; the six Britons and Captain Vargas Bozo.

For the first stage they also had two mule drivers; at the beginning of June 1910 they moved north from La Paz towards the disputed border. Then one of the mule drivers deserted out of fear of Indians, taking the best mule with him. The other, like the second Bolivian officer had done, suddenly complained of feeling ill. He suggested that he leave the expedition at the next town – where he was due to get his first payment – but Fawcett had other ideas. He was already becoming known for valuing and rewarding reliable companions but despising the lazy or incompetent, and he simply sacked the driver on the spot.[xvi] They climbed on without him, crossing the Andes through a pass 15,088 feet up, then dropped down to the river port of Astillero and the start of the real expedition.

Inca Rubber had cut trails through the jungle and they took eight mules with them, heading for the Rio Tambopata. When they reached the Tambopata there was a problem, though. The rainy season should have ended in May, but it was still pouring down. They were stuck at the river for ten days waiting for the water to fall enough to get the mules through. The plan was to follow the Tambopata to its junction with the Heath, collect a supply of food that had been sent there by boat, then continue. It soon became obvious it wasn't going to work.

Apart from Fawcett himself none of the group were used to hacking their way through the jungle, and even with plenty of food and the mules to carry the heavy gear they only managed fifteen miles in ten days. None of them had much experience at driving mules either, and the notoriously stubborn animals were constantly wandering back up their trail or simply standing their ground and refusing to move. Finally Fawcett decided to return to Astillero, abandon the mules and make the whole journey by canoe. He wasn't keen on the idea because they were much more vulnerable to Indian attacks on the river. Although the group was small, six of the seven were trained soldiers, two of them elite light infantrymen, and they could put up a solid defense on land. Out on the river they would be sitting ducks for the Indians' poisoned arrows and blowpipe darts. Fawcett was never deterred by a risk, though, and after the muddy return trip they reorganized themselves and set out again by boat.

The Heath River runs through the Caupolican Swamps, some of the wildest jungle in northern Bolivia, and if possible it was even more infested with menaces than the areas Fawcett had already fought through. Huge areas of deep, clinging mud forced them to climb to the windswept rocky ridges. He called it "an abominable forest, dripping with moisture, the home of malaria and deadly diseases of an obscure South American type" – but over the next four years he returned there again and again. On this first trip there his companions learned the basics of Amazon travel – how to find the shallow water where a canoe could be poled instead of paddled, how to use the wrist to increase the bite of a machete blade and why sleeping on the ant-infested ground was a bad idea – and Fawcett himself discovered new and often painful reasons why hardly anyone lived in the jungle. Among them was the paraponera, or bullet ant; over an inch long, it has the most painful sting of any insect and everyone in the group was bitten at least once.

Then, fifty miles up the Heath, they met a large group of Indians. Knowing that showing hesitation could be dangerous, Fawcett ordered the men to beach their canoes at the village, but immediately they were attacked with bows and even a few old shotguns the Indians had bought or stolen from other travelers. One of the men panicked and jumped into the water, hiding behind a canoe; moments later an arrow smashed through the inch-thick wooden hull, terrifying him even more. Fawcett never named the man – "it was not one of the three non-commissioned officers" (Leigh, Costin, and Todd), he later wrote, and it almost certainly wasn't Henry Manley – but his description of the incident dripped with acid contempt. Moments later they were pinned down behind a mud bank while eight-foot-long shafts thudded into the other side of it, until it "presented the appearance of a plantation of arrows."

Still convinced that opening fire would be more likely to get them killed, Fawcett told Todd to try playing a tune on his accordion – "a somewhat deadly instrument". The arrows and buckshot kept shrieking past overhead. Next he tried shouting out the few words of the local dialect he'd picked up. That was more successful, and an hour and a half into the attack two Indians finally emerged from the jungle and the rain of projectiles faded away. By nightfall the Indians were helping them set up their camp and bringing them bananas, fish and other less practical gifts (including live parrots). One gift Fawcett did appreciate was a red paste that helped repel the ferocious biting insects.

Fawcett observed that the tribespeople, who were known as the Quinaqui, seemed to be "a most intelligent race". While he routinely referred to them as savages, this was common language at the time, and he seems to have quickly developed quite a lot of respect for them. The sudden truce was extremely valuable, because some of the tribe left the village to tell the upstream villages about the approaching explorers and they managed to reach the head of the river with no other attacks. At least there were no other attacks from the Indians, but one night Fawcett, Costin and two others were bitten by vampire bats.

In April 1911 Fawcett gave a presentation at the RGS, describing the expedition. He was already planning the next one and coming to terms with the fact he was now a celebrity. He told everyone that the attention made him feel uncomfortable, but privately he collected newspaper cuttings about himself and pasted them into a journal. He did acknowledge that the publicity would be valuable if it attracted more explorers to the Amazon, which, thanks to rubber, was as valuable in the early 19th century as the Arabian oilfields are today. Unfortunately for him, the RGS was about to pair him up with another celebrity explorer for the next expedition.

On January 1, 1908, Anglo-Irish explorer Ernest Shackleton set out from New Zealand on the decrepit three-masted whaling schooner *Nimrod*;[2] his aim was to lead the first expedition to the South Pole. Towed to the Antarctic Circle by the passenger steamship *Koonya*, on January 14 *Nimrod* hoisted her sails and set off into the iceberg-studded sea of the southern summer. Over the next fifteen months, Shackleton and his men made the first ascent of Mount Erebus, spent the winter preparing their equipment and writing a book (they printed and bound 30 copies of it in their hut) then, on October 29, launched the attempt on the Pole. Shackleton and three companions marched south until January 9 when, short of food, they decided they had to either turn back or die. They were 97.5 miles from the Pole, the closest anyone had ever been, when they abandoned the attempt. On March 4 they reached the ship. Meanwhile, a second team had explored the South Magnetic Pole, which had also never been reached before. The rest of the team stayed in and around the base camp, carrying out experiments. One of them was James Murray.

---

[2] Shackleton had her re-rigged as a barquentine, with square sails on the foremast. *Nimrod* had been fitted with an auxiliary steam engine at some point, and the original gaff foresail's boom threatened to knock her funnel off every time the sail was hauled over.

When Shackleton and his men returned to England in June they were greeted as heroes. They hadn't reached the Pole but they'd come very close, and done a lot of surveying and scientific work in a bleak environment. That made Murray a celebrity, even more than Fawcett was, and there was a lot of public support for him joining the next RGS Amazon expedition.

Murray, born in Glasgow in 1865, was two years older than Fawcett but the difference looked much greater than that. Despite not having been part of Shackleton's actual Polar team, he believed that after surviving the rigors of Antarctica he would have no problems in the jungle, where wind and cold wouldn't be hazards. Fawcett wasn't so sure. He himself was in excellent shape, but Murray looked like a man in his fifties and he'd had a physical breakdown during a long journey round Scotland's lochs to collect specimens. He didn't look fit enough for the jungle. The Scotsman insisted he would be fine though and that limited Fawcett's options. Murray was a scientist – he'd taught himself biology as a teenager, and then made huge contributions to research on freshwater plankton – and a veteran of an expedition that had thrilled the British public. Fawcett was just a surveyor. He didn't even hold a military rank any more – he'd resigned his commission after the last expedition so he could spend all his time on RGS work. Unable to discuss his doubts with Murray he kept them to himself.

If he wasn't sure about Murray, he was a lot more confident in the rest of his team. Sergeant Leigh had suffered badly from insect-borne disease in the final stages of the last trip and his doctor had advised him not to return to the Amazon, but Costin and Manley were as eager to go as Fawcett himself. This would be the smallest expedition yet – four men in total. Fawcett was a lot more confident though. He'd proved that his non-aggressive approach to the Indians worked, and he now spoke more of their language. In late summer 1911 they traveled to Bolivia by ship and train, and made the last preparations. Mules and drivers were hired for the first stage of the trek. On October 4 they set out from San Carlos, a rubber settlement north of Lake Titicaca, and soon they were following the Heath River north.

Murray soon found that exploration in the Amazon was very different from the frozen, almost sterile wastes of Antarctica. Days into the march their camp was attacked by vampire bats; to the biologist's horror the tiny creatures, resembling winged pygmy hamsters with hideous fanged faces, swarmed out of the trees to settle on mules – and men. Vampire bats are acutely sensitive to heat and can use infrared radiation to detect veins beneath the skin of their victims; a second after landing they have located a vein and sliced into it with their razor-like incisors. The vampire's saliva contains anticoagulants that leave the wound bleeding freely long after the bat has fed, and Fawcett was well used to waking up with his hammock soaked in blood from a bite. All of them were bitten as they slept, Fawcett on the head and Costin four times on his right hand. The wounds were small, but in the hot damp jungle infection was a constant hazard.

In fact, in the rainforest, all kinds of bacteria and parasites can thrive in the hothouse conditions. That makes hygiene essential, a fact that Fawcett had patiently explained to Murray. The biologist hadn't paid enough attention though. He thought he knew how to stay clean enough thanks to his Antarctic experience, and he was also struggling with the pace. At each night's camp – Fawcett liked to be ready to march at 7 in the morning and keep the pace up for the next ten hours without breaks – Murray simply collapsed in exhaustion. After snatching a meal he would usually sleep. As days passed he began lagging behind, often reaching the camp an hour or more after the others got there. Tired and aching, he started to let his personal care slip. While the three experienced soldiers cleaned and dried their feet, put on fresh socks, washed and repaired their clothing or stripped off and scrubbed themselves in the river, Murray slumped in his hammock. Tension began to grow between him and Fawcett as he ignored instructions to keep himself clean. All the men were already suffering from bites and minor infections – it was inevitable - but Murray's poor personal administration meant his condition was quickly going downhill.

By the time they'd been in the jungle a week the mules were slowing them down. The drivers had already been paid off at the edge of the forest, and the animals themselves were in a terrible condition. Mules rarely lasted longer than a couple of weeks under the jungle canopy, and it was routine to turn them loose when they couldn't continue. Sometimes they emerged from the forest weeks later, but more often they collapsed and died or fell victim to a jaguar or cougar. Now they stripped the packs off the animals and slung them on their own backs. Fawcett had learned from his previous expeditions and trimmed their equipment to the bare minimum. Each man's load contained his bedding of blankets and hammock, water bottles, spare clothes and cooking equipment. Basic rations filled most of the remaining space. They each had a rifle, revolver and machete, plus a sharp knife. Finally there was the surveying kit. Now, looking at Murray's condition, Fawcett decided not to give him a delicate theodolite or sextant to carry. Instead he handed him his gold pan. The whole region was rich in gold deposits, and every evening, when they camped, Fawcett would scoop up a pan of river gravel and swirl it gently until all that remained was the heaviest sediment. Where flecks of gold gleamed the coordinates would be added to his list of mineral resources. The pan was a vital piece of surveying equipment but, unlike a theodolite, it wouldn't break if the exhausted Murray stumbled and fell.

Now that they were carrying the load themselves, Murray's poor fitness became painfully obvious. On the first day Fawcett had to send Costin back to carry his pack for him, and even then he could barely keep up. On the second day, Murray fell behind almost immediately and finally collapsed exhausted, far behind the others. He wandered off their track looking for an easier route, moving his rucksack by picking it up and throwing it to the front, stumbling a couple of paces to where it had landed, then repeating the process. Fawcett had been right to make sure he wasn't carrying anything delicate. He found a river but managed to drop some of his belongings – including his letters from his wife – into the water. The only food he had was a bag of home-made caramels given to the team by Nina Fawcett and intended to be shared. Now Murray ate half of them and washed them down with unboiled water straight from the river. Finally he lit a cigarette and fell asleep by the water.

When the others camped for the night, at first they expected Murray to stagger in an hour or so behind them. When he didn't, they backtracked some way down the path they'd cleared with their machetes. Still finding no sign they returned to camp, knowing that it was too risky to blunder around the jungle in the dark. The next morning they stacked their kit and patrolled back along their route until they found where Murray had clumsily hacked his way to the river. Minutes later they were dragging the biologist to his feet.

Fawcett was angry by now; Murray was slowing them down, and that was potentially lethal. He made it clear that they had to up the pace, but it made no difference. Every day Murray lagged further behind, then to make matters worse Fawcett caught him eating an extra share of the rations. He started to throw away equipment – his spare clothes, his hammock and finally, to Fawcett's anger, the gold pan. Instead of making it easier the loss of so much gear accelerated his decline. Now Murray had to sleep on the ground at night and woke up every morning covered in a mass of ant bites. The others were washing clothes in the river so they always had a relatively clean set to wear but Murray's garments deteriorated into a stinking, shredded mess, slimy with sweat and jungle grime.

They were all suffering. Costin had contracted leishmaniasis from a sandfly bite; his face was a mass of sores and he was half delirious with fever. Manley also had a fever and his sweat-soaked body seemed to be burning away his flesh. Fawcett had been parasitized by botfly larvae, which were burrowing their way under the skin of his arms. Apart from that, he was in good health, though; he seemed to have an inhuman resistance to jungle disease. With his clothes constantly repaired and as clean as he could keep them, his feet encased in tall, well-broken leather boots and his head protected by a wide-brimmed Terai hat the flies had few chances to attack him. The maggots in his arms itched but he knew they wouldn't do any real harm, so he left them alone until the flies hatched and the wounds healed.

But Murray was a mess. He had also been targeted by the botflies but in his filthy rags he was much more vulnerable. Then, ignoring Fawcett's warnings, he tried to poison the maggots by flushing the wounds with anything he could find – lime, potassium permanganate, tobacco juice. Some of the maggots died – and began to rot under Murray's skin, causing horrific infections. Dozens more kept munching their way through his body. His right arm and knee were worst affected. Counting them, he found over fifty parasites around the elbow alone.

There were other dramas. Fawcett had brought two dogs with him, but cougars stalked the rainforest and the big cats are particularly drawn to dogs. One night they were woken by a horrible scream as one of the hounds was killed and carried off. Soon after, the other drowned as they crossed a river. During another river crossing Murray nearly overturned the crude raft that carried their gear. All the time the biologist's health steadily failed. Finally he became delirious and couldn't go on. He was barely conscious enough to notice as the others huddled round the fire discussing whether they should simply abandon him or leave him with a lethal dose of opium tablets. Then Fawcett made a surprising decision.

It had always been understood that abandonment was the fate of anyone who couldn't go on, but looking at the map Fawcett had seen that there were rubber plantations within a few days' walk of their route. He didn't like Murray and was furious that the man's weakness and poor discipline had slowed them down so much, but when it came to it he couldn't leave him to die. With Manley he set off to look for help, leaving Costin to guard Murray. The former infantryman was in a bad way himself, but he handled the task easily enough. His patient needed to be physically restrained, and Costin took his revolver from him in case Murray decided to use it. Before anything worse could happen Fawcett and Hanley returned, bringing a prospector and his mule. The man had agreed to take Murray to the nearest town. Now Fawcett gave him some cash to pay for food and whatever medical treatment he could find and said a stiff, angry farewell. Costin lingered a moment, pointing at Murray's bloated, stinking leg. "You know that knee of yours is far worse than you think?" he said,[xvii] then the three former soldiers melted into the jungle.

Costin and Hanley were both extremely ill, but they had an iron determination that matched Fawcett's own and they were determined to survey as much of the expedition's route as they could. They had the experience to know that however bad they felt they weren't in any immediate danger as long as they looked after themselves and completed the trek quickly. All three of them agreed that they'd never see Murray alive again, though. The Scotsman just hadn't had what it took, they thought, and his body had been so riddled with infection that he couldn't possibly survive. When they finally emerged from the jungle and marched into the Peruvian town of Cojata the first thing Fawcett did was organize a search, then he sent a telegram to the RGS to tell them Murray was missing, presumed dead.

But he wasn't dead. In early 1912 he reached La Paz, having been nursed back to health by a Bolivian farmer and his family, and immediately launched a furious assault on Fawcett's reputation. He'd been driven to collapse, he complained; Fawcett's tyrannical leadership had almost killed him.

The RGS had sent the expedition out there; they were concerned at what this public attack would do to their reputation. As soon as they could they interviewed the three explorers. Costin and Manley both backed Fawcett's version, which was that Murray was undisciplined and disruptive, and had been pushed hard in an effort to save his life. Studying the evidence they concluded that Fawcett's version was more believable and that he'd done all he could for Murray in a very tight spot. Nevertheless, they urged him to resolve the argument. Murray had powerful friends, they warned, including the national hero Shackleton. An open fight with him could be very bad for his reputation. At the same time Murray threatened to sue Fawcett, but the Society pressured him into dropping the idea. A century later, it's impossible to say for sure which version of the 1911 expedition is true – was Fawcett an inhuman slave driver, or was Murray stubborn, willful and unreliable? But perhaps we can guess.

In 1913 James Murray joined an expedition to the Arctic. After their ship sank in the ice and the crew set up a temporary camp on shore, Murray led a mutiny against the captain, stole a sled, and vanished towards the coast of Siberia with three other mutineers. He was never seen again.

Chapter 7: Fawcett At War

Fawcett, Manley and Costin returned to the Amazon in late 1913, this time to chart the hilly borders of the Caupolican region. The jungle was even more desolate than any they'd been through before, but in a series of shorter expeditions the three, along with another man named Brown, mapped huge areas of it. Perhaps more importantly to Fawcett, he spent time with the Indians, learning their herbal medicines and tribal legends. Many of the tribes came to trust the small band of adventurers and, despite some tense encounters, they only broke his no-violence rule once. About to be overrun by a group of Indians – a hostile group the other tribes had warned them about – he finally gave in to Costin's appeals and allowed weapons to be used. In a last, desperate attempt to avoid bloodshed he ordered his men to fire warning shots over their heads or into the ground. The pragmatic Costin felt it was too late for that and blasted one of the attackers through the stomach. The rest fled, and the expedition continued.

One of the things that was beginning to fascinate Fawcett was the idea of a lost ancient city concealed deep within the jungle. On the 1913-1914 expeditions he had been amazed to find tribes who cultivated maize, sweet potatoes, bananas and other crops in large plantations hacked from the jungle. They were also cannibals who ate their own dead, a practice Fawcett described sympathetically in his presentations later, but this scale of agriculture made him think. Every Indian group he'd met so far had survived by hunting, foraging and perhaps a few small vegetable plots. If major farming was possible in the forest, however, perhaps in the past there had been cities – and perhaps they were still there to be found. If there were cities there it was likely they were rich, because his nightly panning was finding a tantalizingly high concentration of gold in the river sediments.

Now, in his journal, Fawcett began scribbling down his theories about the nature and possible location of these hypothetical cities. He was increasingly drawn to the idea of searching for one. Of course, that was an expedition he'd need to fund himself, because the RGS was unlikely to pay for him to go searching for an El Dorado-style fable, and he didn't have the money. Before he could find a solution the politics of his far-away home in Europe dramatically changed his plans.

The First World War began on July 28, 1914. At first the optimists in Britain believed that, between France's powerful army and the Royal Navy's domination of the seas, it would all be over by Christmas. They were in for a crushing disappointment. Traditional infantry and cavalry attacks were stopped dead by the power of the machine gun, which had been used in colonial wars for decades but had never been deployed *en masse* in a full scale war before. The carnage was unbelievable, and within weeks the opposing armies were sheltering in trenches along an almost immobile front line. One of the few weapons that could get at dug-in troops was the heavy gun, and the Royal Artillery began to expand dramatically. When the news of the war reached Bolivia, the surveying was quickly abandoned. Brown elected to stay in South America but the other three returned to England as fast as they could. Manley enlisted in the Army, Costin returned to the Rifle Brigade and was sent to the front, and Fawcett asked the gunners for his commission back. He was instantly accepted.

For the British Army, the worst of the war's fighting took place in Flanders, on the flat, wet clay farmland east of the Somme River. More than 4 million British troops fought there, sometimes up to 2 million at a time, and a mass of artillery was assembled to support them. The RA grew to more than four times its prewar size and tactics changed radically to suit the new, heavier guns. Before 1914, artillery had mostly fired over open sights at visible targets. Now increased ranges meant fire control had to be used, relying on observers, rangefinders and map predicted fire. In fact the skills required were very similar to heavy coastal artillery – which Fawcett had worked with for most of his military career.

Fawcett rejoined the Army as a major commanding a battery of QF (Quick Firing) 18-Pounder field guns, handy and fast-firing 3.3-inch weapons that could throw shells out to five miles but were most effective in direct fire at shorter ranges. Because their rapid fire could rip an attack to pieces with shrapnel shells they were often pushed right up to the front. Fawcett – along with his enthusiastic young lieutenant, Cecil Lyne – placed their guns within a few hundred yards of the German trenches so they could sweep every inch of no man's land.

The French and Belgian civilians who'd farmed the fertile land of the battlefield had left years before so it was unusual to see anyone except British or Empire troops, and occasionally the Germans as they advanced. It was certainly unusual to see a man in a French steel helmet and ankle-length Russian fur greatcoat wandering around a ruined village, apparently looking for a good observation post. Fawcett checked the loads in his heavy Webley revolver, climbed out of the trench and challenged him. The possibility that the man was a German spy was a worrying one and many soldiers would have shot first and asked questions later. Perhaps remembering his policy of not shooting at the Amazonian tribesmen, Fawcett didn't; instead he introduced himself and asked the stranger's name. "Lieutenant Colonel Churchill, 6th Royal Scots Fusiliers," was the reply. Satisfied, Fawcett thanked him, buttoned the flap on his holster and jogged back to his guns. Winston Churchill lit a cigar and continued his leisurely inspection of the devastated houses.

As new units were created, officers were needed to command them, and higher ranks started to be handed out. Promoted to Lieutenant Colonel, Fawcett now commanded a whole brigade of guns. An artillery brigade was different from an infantry brigade, which consisted of three or more battalions and might also include cavalry, engineers and artillery; Fawcett's command was about the same size as a battalion and got its name from the fact that batteries of four to eight guns each were "brigaded" together. Before the war the batteries would usually work independently, each one being attached to an infantry or cavalry unit, but to dump enough explosives on an enemy trench their fire had to be massed. By late 1916 Fawcett controlled nine batteries of heavy guns, enough firepower to utterly devastate hundreds of square yards every minute. His job was counter-battery fire for the British Army's VI Corps, holding the front near Arras. There were three divisions of troops in VI Corps, almost 80,000 men in total, and except when they left the trenches for an attack the biggest danger they faced was German artillery. Fawcett's job as Counter-Battery Colonel was to locate enemy artillery firing at the Corps trenches and destroy it with his 54 modern 60-Pounder (5-inch) guns. The 60-Pounder could throw a high explosive shell over seven miles, and with his batteries spaced out along the Corps front he could quickly hammer any German guns his spotters detected. One question that's been asked is, did he actually use his spotters? There's controversy about Fawcett's performance during the war. His air of mystery, and his family's connections with spiritualism and mysticism, has bred many strange stories. The tale of how he might have found targets is one of the strangest.

As artillery ranges opened out, new technology was being trialed to help spotters locate enemy artillery. A heavy gun firing created a huge flash, which would often be visible on low clouds (and it often rains in Flanders) or even the smoke built up from their own propellant. A spotter with a modified theodolite could take a bearing on the flash then, using a microphone linked to a modified camera, measure the time interval between the flash and the sound of the shot reaching the spotting bunker. It wasn't perfect – in fact it wasn't very reliable at all – but it was getting better rapidly and often it gave the best information available about where the 60-Pounders should drop their shells.

According to at least one account from the trenches Fawcett refused to use it.[xviii] He would only order fire on targets that could be directly seen from the British lines, or that he had detected using a Ouija board. It's a surprising story. Fawcett was developing some unusual ideas by this point but they mostly involved lost South American civilizations. There's nothing in his own writing about using a Ouija to make decisions. It's not completely impossible, though. His brother had become a close friend of famous spiritualist (and notorious crank) Helena Blavatsky, to the point where he helped her with her best-known book. *The Secret Doctrine* lays out the principles of Blavatsky's occult beliefs and a highly eccentric history of the human race. She claimed its contents had been revealed to her by "mahatmas" – highly evolved superhuman Indian mystics. In fact, Edward Fawcett wrote most of it. Among other things Blavatsky was an enthusiastic Ouija practitioner, and it's very likely that Fawcett had been exposed to it. Did he use one for plotting artillery fire though?

Probably not. Popular history has a low opinion of First World War British generals, but in reality most of them were highly professional. Thrown into a war unlike anything that had ever been experienced before they adapted relatively quickly, and the Army of 1916 was a professional and fast-evolving organization. Fawcett wasn't working in isolation; he had a fire planning staff working around him and answered to the Commander Royal Artillery, a brigadier, at Corps HQ. It wouldn't have been long before such an outlandish fire control system reached the ears of his superiors and that would have been the end of his career in counter-battery fire. Instead he kept his job and, after the war, had the opportunity to stay in the RA.

It must have been tempting. After the war, the RGS found itself short of funds, and the number of expeditions was scaled back sharply. He wouldn't be able to rely on the Society to send him back to the jungle. At the same time he was now in his early 50s and didn't know any career apart from exploring and artillery. Resigning his commission again would leave him with no reliable income and little hope of finding a good job. However, the lure of the jungle was too strong. In 1919 he returned to England, Nina and his three children.

He was delighted to spend time with the children again, especially Jack. Brian was less athletic and preferred reading, and Fawcett didn't quite know what to say to Joan, but as always, he felt a strong connection to Jack. Now fifteen, the boy was fit, strong and confident, and keen to start sharing his father's adventures. Along with his best friend Raleigh Rimmell, he constantly had to be bailed out of trouble his high spirits – and sometimes recklessness – had got him into.

Fawcett's own streak of recklessness soon made itself felt. Life in post-war England bored him intensely and he was determined to return to South America. In 1920 he made the first step; he'd managed to save some money during the war and now he used it to move the family to Jamaica. By coincidence, Rimmell was already there; his father had died and his mother had moved there to live with a distant cousin. Jack was delighted, and soon found work on a nearby fruit plantation. After work he and Rimmell would plan their own expeditions; they just needed to get the experience they would need. It wasn't long before the chance appeared.

Since hearing the first rumors in 1911, Fawcett had been increasingly obsessed with the lost city he called Z. He'd spend endless hours working with maps of the region, both official ones and those he'd created himself. Old journals from expeditions going back to the 16th century were studied in a meticulous search for clues. Whenever he could afford it he traveled to Brazil to examine archaeological sites and official records. Finally, he decided he had enough information to narrow down the search area to what could be covered in a single expedition, and he started drawing up his plans.

But this time he was on his own. Hanley had died of a heart attack shortly after the war, probably as a delayed effect of his earlier jungle fevers. Even the indomitable Costin had abandoned exploring; after returning from the front when the war ended he had met a woman and was now married. Whatever Fawcett did, it would be without his two most experienced and reliable companions. He was going to have to arrange his own funding and find another team.

Late in 1920, Fawcett traveled to Brazil to beg the government for funding. He thought, correctly, that they would be interested in finding out more about the jungle interior. The South American rubber industry had collapsed since the war, and the country was desperately searching for something to rebuild the shattered economy. If Fawcett could survey the last stretches of uncharted jungle he might find resources that would bring back prosperity to the region.

There was a trust issue, though, because Fawcett was British and, worse, RGS. There was a reason the rubber industry had failed and it certainly wasn't because nobody wanted rubber any more. South America was a natural rubber producing region, but the industry was incredibly inefficient. Plantations were really just stretches of jungle with a high density of rubber trees, and workers – many of them slaves and all of them appallingly treated – had to struggle through the forest to tap the latex from the trees. Collection, transport and the constant replacement of workers all pushed the price up, but as rubber only grows naturally in South America, the world had no choice but to pay. Then in 1876, Sir Henry Wickham arrived in Brazil.

Sir Henry was an English explorer and a member of the Society. He also had a keen eye for crops that could expand the British Empire's already booming economy, and he was a good judge of climate. Walking around the rubber-producing areas of Brazil he decided that the temperature, humidity and rainfall weren't that different from many parts of the Empire, especially in the Far East. He discreetly collected 70,000 rubber tree seeds, labelled the boxes as "Biological specimens" and had them shipped to London. There they were taken to the Royal Botanical Gardens at Kew and handed over to the nursery staff. Kew managed to get 2,400 seeds to sprout, and within months they were on ships heading to Malaya, Ceylon, India, Nigeria and various other tropical corners of the Empire. It was the late 1880s before commercial production began because there weren't enough trees. More seeds had to be grown and planted. The plantations slowly grew, though, and the first loads of latex went to market. By the early 20th century British colonies, especially Malaya and the Indian state of Kerala, were turning out an increasing flood of rubber. The Brazilians, realizing too late what had happened, were furious.

South America just couldn't compete. The new plantations were efficiently laid out on cleared, fertile soil; mile after mile of healthy rubber trees, all easy to access and regularly harvested by skilled workers who found the task easy after the intricate work of harvesting coffee or tea. The crop could be loaded straight into trains and brought to harbor by the extensive Imperial rail network, then transported anywhere in the world by the huge British merchant fleet. Prices nosedived to a fraction of what they'd been and cheap rubber goods started appearing in every European and American home. Unable to sell their suddenly overpriced product, the Brazilian rubber industry fell apart with shocking speed. By 1920, almost nothing remained.

It was too late to do anything about rubber but the Brazilians were worried that if Fawcett found anything else of value he would somehow manage to steal it for Britain. They agreed to fund the expedition on condition that a Brazilian explorer, General Cândido Rondon, go with him. Fawcett was reluctant; Rondon was an experienced explorer and had a higher military rank than Fawcett himself had held (even though he'd dropped the "Lieutenant" from his rank once he returned to South America and called himself simply Colonel Fawcett) and would naturally expect to be the real leader of the expedition. If he wanted funding, though, there was little choice. In a personal audience with the president of Brazil he explained the evidence for the city of Z, and managed to convince him it was worth looking for. The funding was agreed and he went looking for men. Finally he settled on two: an enormous Australian, Lewis Brown, and American ornithologist Ernest Holt. Holt dreamed of being a naturalist and idolized Charles Darwin; Brown was simply a rough adventurer. Neither was the equal of the dead Manley or of Costin, now peacefully at home in England, but they were what he could get. Carefully budgeting the Brazilian grant he began buying the expedition's equipment. Then he had a stroke of luck.

The Brazilian government was having serious trouble balancing their budget and the bean counters decided that sending a general into the jungle after a lost city was a luxury they couldn't afford. The expedition could go ahead on a reduced budget, they said, but the Brazilian army wouldn't be sending anyone. That suited Fawcett just fine.

Brown and Holt didn't. In mid-November they set off from Cuiaba, heading northeast into the basin of the Xingú River where he believed the lost city lay. Within days they were in trouble. Brown was six feet five and heavily muscled – he was a skilled boxer – but mentally he was nowhere near as tough. Isolated in the Green Hell, his mind quickly began to turn on him. In the second week of the expedition it was clear he was heading for a serious breakdown, so Fawcett gave him a few days' rations and sent him back to Cuiba.

They'd brought animals with them – two oxen to carry their load, two horses and two dogs. Now the vampire bats and swarming insect life began to weaken them. Holt was suffering too, sickening from insect bites. Even Fawcett himself, it seemed, was no longer immune to the jungle. Bites in his leg became infected, and he could only limp painfully. When they could, they rode. But the animals were going down faster than the men. An ox, infested by botfly maggots, collapsed and died. One of the dogs got too weak to go on and was shot. A horse drowned crossing a river. Finally the last horse stopped, trembling, and refused to go any further. Fawcett tried to coax it onwards, but finally it collapsed. With the compassion for suffering animals that Holt had already been impressed by, the aging explorer drew his Mauser automatic and shot it between the eyes. Then, exhausted, they made camp. Fawcett searched out dry grass and bark to light a fire, and the two men shared a crude meal. Then they discussed their options. They were stark. Abandon Holt, or give up and go back. It was an option, but perhaps Fawcett was mellowing as he got older. If he left Holt the young American would die, and even if he was impatient with his slow pace he felt a certain loyalty to him for coming this far. Then there was the fact that his own leg was swollen and half crippled. It wasn't likely to recover in the jungle and the chances were that he, too, would collapse before too long. He made his decision; in the morning they loaded their gear onto the last ox and headed back the way they had come.

Within weeks they were planning another attempt, but then Fawcett began to grow paranoid. He started to suspect Holt was working for a rival RGS expedition, and decided to do without him. Holt was stunned and disappointed; he had a contract that covered the next expedition, and had been counting on it to launch a scientific career. Many of his friends were relieved, though. They had heard of Fawcett's reputation as a hard charger and felt it was only a matter of time before something went terribly wrong.

Fawcett seemed determined to prove them right. Unable to find any companions he felt he could rely on he made an incredible decision. Selling off whatever assets he could spare, including part of his Army pension fund, he replaced the equipment lost on the last attempt and spent what was left on food and ammunition. Then he traveled to Bahia, plotted a route to where he was sure the lost city waited for him, and in August 1921 he set out into the jungle once more.

Alone.

Chapter 8: The Last Gamble

His experience over five previous expeditions had given Fawcett immense confidence in his own abilities. Even at 53 years old he was very fit. He had phenomenally quick reactions – once he managed to jump clear of a striking viper. He knew more about the Indians and their culture than any other European, and of course he seemed almost immune to tropical disease. Now, in late middle age, he could add an immense depth of practical experience to his other skills. Even so, to enter the jungle alone was a terrible risk. If he fell ill or had an accident there would be nobody to help. Despite his skill and weapons he would be horribly vulnerable. At night he'd have to sleep alone; if hostile Indians or a predator attacked there would be nobody to come to help. Even Fawcett himself knew it was an insane risk, but as he wrote, it might be his last chance to find Z. He was getting older, and didn't have the funding he'd once been able to rely on. He also had rivals. American doctor Alexander Hamilton Rice had launched a series of well-funded but unsuccessful expeditions to find Z, and was preparing to try again. In fact, Fawcett suspected Holt might have been working with his fellow American. He couldn't stand the thought of being beaten to his goal, and it was that desperation that forced him into his mad gamble.

And of course he failed. It took two whole months, but eventually the jungle wore down even Fawcett's iron will and he turned around. It's remarkable that he made it out at all; as he plodded wearily back along his trail he was low on food, exhausted and dispirited. When he finally emerged from the trees in early December it looked as if his long career as an explorer was finally over; Percy Fawcett had been beaten by the jungle at last. But he wasn't ready to give in just yet.

It was obvious that he couldn't do it on his own, but he didn't have the money to hire anyone to go with him. His reputation was still a powerful draw, and there were people willing to go with him, but in his opinion – and it was probably correct – most of them were unsuitable. He even had an offer from T.E. Lawrence – "Lawrence of Arabia" – but quickly turned it down. After his experience with Murray he was wary of anyone whose experience was in such a radically different environment. As he said, "Excellent work in the Near East does no infer the ability or willingness to hump a 60 pound pack, live for a year in the forest, suffer from legions of insects and accept the conditions which I would impose." Lawrence, he believed, wasn't up to the challenge of the Amazon. But he thought he knew who was.

Even before he set out on his own he'd been wondering about his older son, Jack. Jack was fit and adventurous. He was undoubtedly loyal. Would he make a suitable companion? Fawcett thought he would, although in 1921 he was still in his teens. Now he settled more firmly on the idea. When Jack was a bit older, he decided, he would take him along, and by 1922 he felt the young man was ready. Nina didn't object. She had an almost religious belief in Fawcett's abilities and believed Jack must have inherited them. She was also fully committed to her husband's quest; if he had allowed it she would happily have gone herself. Unlike most women at the time she worked constantly to stay fit and had taught herself to shoot and live outdoors. When Fawcett raised the idea with his son Nina was supportive; it was down to Jack.

Jack was delighted, and only had one condition. If he went, then Raleigh Rimmell had to come too. He and Rimmell had spent so long planning adventures that he couldn't imagine actually going on one without his friend. Fawcett contemplated it. Rimmell was less dedicated to exploration – he wanted to be a movie star – but he was also young, fit and confident. If he agreed to follow the rules he should do well, and a party of three had an extra margin of safety. After all, if he could have set out with Costin and Hanley he would have been perfectly happy.

Rimmell had had no luck with the film industry and was working in tedious jobs; perhaps the glamor of an Amazon trek would help him break into Hollywood. Mrs. Rimmell's worries seemed unnecessary, though. Fawcett simply didn't have the cash to mount the expedition. While he had friends and supporters at the RGS, none of them were able or willing to stump up the cash, and his own resources were at an end. He even had to sell off some antiques to pay his RGS membership. Then, in late 1924, he met George Lynch.

Lynch was a former war correspondent and was well connected in the media, both in his native Britain and the USA. He was also fascinated by the idea of lost cities. If Fawcett let him tell the story of the expedition, he promised, he'd find the money for it. And he did. There wasn't a lot of cash up front – most of the deal involved payment for story rights – but some trickled in, and even the RGS finally scraped up some. Mostly they were motivated by the fear of a British explorer being seen to rely on America for support, but they did give him what support they could. That was just as well, because Lynch managed to blow $1,000 on whiskey and prostitutes during a huge bender in New York, but slowly the project gained attention and more money came in. The final total was about $10,000, just enough to buy the supplies and equipment they would need. In December 1924 Fawcett and Jack sailed for New York to meet Rimmell, and by early February they were in Rio de Janeiro. The last preparations began.

More than any of Fawcett's previous journeys, this one set off to a huge explosion of media attention. Jack was amused. Fawcett no doubt complained about the coverage but snipped out the best articles for his scrapbook. In the meantime, he put together the final pieces of equipment. The three took a train to São Paulo, where they visited a snake farm and collected a large supply of antivenin. Jack and Rimmell were awed at the wilderness they saw on their journey, and reacted with boyish high spirits.

That might have worried Fawcett, as a hint of problems ahead. Once, the young men saw alligators on a river bank and tried to shoot them from a moving train. It was irresponsible, and clashed badly with Fawcett's own strict rules about the use of firearms. They carried on, though, switching trains then catching a riverboat heading for Cuiaba – the end of the line.

Cuiaba would be the start of their trek, but they were in no hurry to leave. Fawcett wanted to start getting his young companions accustomed to the climate and terrain. They had to break in their boots; his own were shaped and softened by years of wear, but theirs were stiff leather that, until they'd walked miles in them, cut and blistered their feet. Once the boots were ready they had to wait longer until their feet had healed; burst blisters would get infected quickly in the forest. Pack animals had to be bought and acclimated to the insects, in the hope they'd build up resistance to disease and stay alive longer. Most importantly, they had to wait until the rainy season ended. Fawcett himself was happy to go into the jungle at any time, but he knew it was even more dangerous than ever in the rains and didn't want to take the risk with the others.

On April 19 the sun was shining on Cuiaba. It was time. Fawcett visited a German diplomat he knew and asked him to send a final message to Nina, Brian and Joan. Then he returned to his rented house to pack his kit. When he awoke next morning they just had to load the packs on the mules and go.

A crowd gathered to watch the expedition move out. Fawcett had hired porters and guides to go with them for the first hundred miles, where the real jungle began. The first stage was much easier, ideal for the boys to gain experience, and the porters would let them cover it at a steady pace without eating into the supplies they'd need once they were on their own. As they headed north they visited villagers and ranchers, discussing the expedition and also picking up news that could help them – reports of disease, flooding and Indian activity could prove vital.

It wasn't a trouble-free journey. In letters home, Jack complained about Rimmell, who he said was lazy and nervous. They were plagued by mosquitoes and even Fawcett wrote that "Years tell, in spite of the enthusiasm". Rimmell himself seemed to be losing enthusiasm for the adventure. None of them wanted to back out now, though; they pushed on. Finally they reached Dead Horse Camp, where he'd admitted defeat and turned back with Holt. The bleached bones of the horse he'd shot there were still visible, polished by ants and slowly sinking into the leaf mold. This was the end of known territory. The Brazilian guides and porters were paid off and the three explorers loaded their packs with the essentials they would carry the rest of the way.

Fawcett asked Rimmell for a private word. Out of Jack's earshot he suggested the young man return to Cuiaba with the guides; he didn't feel he had the mental or physical toughness for the expedition, and was worried he would slow them down. Loyalty to Jack made Rimmell refuse. Reluctantly Fawcett accepted. In the morning he handed a packet to the guides with their last letters, and shouldered his heavy rucksack. Then the Brazilians watched as the three Englishmen, led by the tall, lean figure of Fawcett, struck out into the untamed forest.

They were never seen again.

Chapter 9: A Mysterious Legacy

The plan had been to find the lost city of Z, then spend anywhere up to a year exploring it. Fawcett had packed five years' worth of essential medicines and as much ammunition, salt and other necessities as he could. He could live off the land, and was probably more capable of surviving in the jungle than any other explorer. Nobody worried when the expedition hadn't returned by the end of 1925, or even the end of 1926, but when the rains ended in March 1927 and the three men were still missing people started to suspect that something had gone wrong.

The first attempt to find them was launched in 1928 by a fellow RGS member, the Anglo-American test pilot and explorer George Dyott. After a grueling trek into the jungle Dyott returned with a conclusive tale of Fawcett's death. Having found some pieces of equipment in a Kalapalo Indian village he decided that the local chief had murdered Fawcett's party and stolen their supplies. There were problems with the story, though. The items he'd seen could easily have come from the 1920 expedition with Holt, or been given as gifts – which is what the Indian chief said they had been. Dyott's main evidence was his conviction that the chief was untrustworthy, and that was weakened by the fact the same chief had happily assisted his own group. Finally Dyott's star witness, a Brazilian guide called Bernandino who claimed to have been with the lost group, hadn't been mentioned in any of Fawcett's last letters – the real guides had been. Nina Fawcett and many others rejected his conclusions and the mystery remained unsolved.

Over the next years – and then the next decades – many increasingly wild tales came out of the jungle. Some travelers claimed to have met Fawcett himself, either being held captive by Indian tribes (one said he was being worshipped as a god and had fathered 200 children) or living in the lost city itself. Others found evidence of his death, or his continued survival. Some real clues did appear – in 1933 a compass that had belonged to Fawcett was found not far from where he had disappeared, but it was in good condition and obviously hadn't been lying in the jungle for eight years. Perhaps someone, an Indian maybe, had found it and carried it, then later lost it himself. Or perhaps Fawcett still lived, somewhere out there in the Green Hell.

More expeditions were launched. A Swiss who said he'd seen an emaciated Fawcett in an Indian village hired a boat and set off up the Xingú River. He was never seen again. English actor Albert de Winton spent nine months searching then returned nine months later, empty handed and half starved. Undaunted he tried again – and vanished forever. Years later Brazilian officials found out he had been murdered by Indians, although he'd already gone mad in the jungle. Peter Fleming, brother of the James Bond author Ian, launched an attempt and failed. By 1934, a dozen expeditions had gone into the jungle on Fawcett's trail and several of them hadn't come back. Exasperated, the Brazilians banned amateurs from making the attempt. They were ignored, and would-be heroes kept heading into the jungle to find the enigmatic colonel and his two young companions.

The Second World War happened and fifty million died. The world changed. The Cold War terrified us all for four decades. Through it all people kept shouldering a pack and rifle, and setting out to find Fawcett. Harrowing tales of animals, fever and Indians emerged from the jungle; they were carried by starving survivors, Indians, and even once by a carrier pigeon. Nobody found a trace of the missing explorers, and some of the searchers – up to a hundred by some estimates - failed to come back.

In 1951, a Brazilian Indian rights activist, Orlando Villas-Boâs, came out of the jungle with a skeleton he said was Fawcett's. He claimed to have spoken to the Kalapalo village where Fawcett had last been seen, and to have been told by eyewitnesses that having lost the gifts they planned to hand out, and already suffering badly from illness, the party had been murdered by the villagers. The younger men had been thrown in the river and the more highly respected Fawcett had been buried. Villas-Boâs claimed that analysis of the bones proved they were the colonel's. A Danish explorer visited the village in the 1960s and reported that the Kalapalo confirmed the story.

Brian Fawcett didn't believe the story, and after a dispute with Villas-Boâs arranged to have the bones examined again, in London. The pathologist reported that they came from a man much shorter than Fawcett had been. The skull also had a number of teeth, including one that Fawcett had lost; the report drily noted that "these human remains are not those of Colonel Fawcett, whose spare denture is fortunately available for comparison".[xix]

The Kalapalo seemed to be the key to the mystery, but they finally got fed up with all the attention. In 1996 an American father and son expedition was taken hostage and only released after handing over all their equipment and arranging a $30,000 ransom. However, by 1998 they were willing to talk again and told British explorer Benedict Allen, and the BBC crew with him, that the bones Villas-Boâs found hadn't been Fawcett's. They also denied having had anything to do with the expedition's disappearance.

American author David Grann visited the Kalapalos in 2005 and came back with his own conclusions, reported in an article and then a book. His conclusions are interesting but contradict several earlier accounts; without more information it's hard to say if his central claim – that Fawcett left the Kalapalo village heading east and was murdered by another tribe – is correct. What's certain is that Grann won't be the last person to go in search of answers. Even now, nearly 90 years after Fawcett disappeared into the jungle, there are people contemplating following in his footsteps in the hope that they will be the one to, finally, solve the mystery. And some of them won't come back.

Even if people ever do stop searching for Fawcett, it's unlikely his impact on our culture will fade any time soon. Although the character of Indiana Jones was officially based on the archetypal heroic explorer from 1920s fiction, those archetypes themselves drew heavily on Fawcett. The idea of the lean, competent adventurer hacking his way into the jungle in search of an ancient mystery resonates very strongly with anyone who's studied the tale of Fawcett and his lost city.

Chapter 10: Will We Ever Know?

So what really happened to Colonel Percy Fawcett and his two young followers? Without hard evidence it's impossible to say, and the chances of any evidence being found are now approximately zero. Their bodies will have been processed into the jungle biomass long ago, and much of their clothing and equipment will have disintegrated. Even items that remain will be buried unless someone else has picked them up, in which case they can offer few clues as to what happened sometime in 1925 or 1926. There are a few possibilities though, some of them backed up by hints that have emerged from the region in the decades since the mystery began.

One of the most popular theories is that the trio was killed by Indians. There's no doubt that the Indian peoples of the Amazon are suspicious of outsiders, often with good reason. Fawcett had an amazing ability to relate with them though; in all his years in the region he only had to resort to violence once, where many other explorers were driven out of the jungle – even killed – by Indian attacks. Villas-Boâs claimed to have been told that the group had offended the Kalalpolas in various ways, including urinating in the river upstream from their village and slapping a curious child, but it's hard to believe this. Perhaps one of the younger men could have done so, but before approaching a village Fawcett would have told them in the strongest terms how to behave. He was well aware of the local customs and the risks of violating them, and there's little chance he would have taken any risks if he didn't trust his companions to follow the rules.

David Grann reports that the Kalapalos warned Fawcett not to go east from their village, because the tribes there were dangerous, but that he insisted on going anyway. According to the story, they watched the smoke from his evening fires for five days, further away each time, until on the sixth day there was no sign of it; that, supposedly, is when the disaster occurred. This is a much more believable version of events but still not perfect. The tale of the absent campfire smoke is far too neat. Smoke from a fire doesn't always ascend easily through the jungle canopy, and even when it does it can be easily obscured in the damp tropical haze. Still, that can be put down to creative storytelling. Grann's version has to be at least as likely as any other.

It's certainly more likely than the wild claims that Fawcett never intended to come back, but planned to found a spiritualist commune deep in the jungle. This is a popular theory among some fans of the esoteric, but it doesn't seem plausible. Fawcett certainly didn't object to the idea of "going native" but would he really have walked away from his beloved wife to do it? It just doesn't seem believable.

It's natural for people to want a dramatic conclusion to any tale, and Indian attacks or a long life as a jungle mystic certainly appeal to that instinct, but what many seem to be overlooking is just where the party disappeared. The Amazon rainforest is immense, and one of the most difficult environments imaginable. The native tribes still suffer from extremely poor life expectancy thanks to disease, animals and malnutrition; scraping a living from the jungle is incredibly difficult. It's even more difficult if you're constantly moving, trying to reach an objective instead of staying in one place and doing your best to cultivate the meager food resources. That makes it very likely that the Fawcett expedition was simply overcome by the environment. The younger members didn't have any experience of the jungle, and we know from their last letters that Raleigh Rimmell in particular was already suffering by the time they left Dead Horse Camp. Both he and Jack were unused to the insects, the parasites and the constant risk of infection; either one could have been quickly crippled. The sensible thing for Fawcett to have done would have been to abandon them and press on, but this is where his choice of companions would have worked against him. Twice in his career he had already faced the option of abandonment – Murray and, later, Holt – and both times he'd balked at actually doing it. What are the chances he would have given his son a handful of opium tablets or a revolver with one loaded chamber, wished him farewell then walked away into the trees? They're probably not high. He might have been more inclined to leave Rimmell but Jack may not have wanted to do that to his lifelong friend. The three entered the jungle together and it's likely they stayed together until the end.

What could have happened is that one or both of the young men fell victim to fever or infection, and Fawcett finally took the decision to give up and go back. That wouldn't have been an easy step to take; if he failed this time he would probably never have found the funding to try again, so he would have pushed on relentlessly until there was simply no option. Then, probably with the last of his pack animals sick, dying or already gone, he'd have been faced with the challenge of evacuating someone back to the tenuous safety of the last Indian villages.

Two people could, just, carry a third through the jungle but it would have been a slow process. The jungle would have started to grow back over their trail in a matter of days, so machete work would have been needed to clear the track again before going back to pick up the casualty. The extra effort needed would have run down the food supplies, which were already trimmed to the bone. And even Fawcett himself, while still awesomely fit, was no longer quite as resilient as he'd once been. Sooner or later the other youth would have collapsed too, and when that happened the escape was over. Fawcett might have trudged on for another day or two with Jack over his shoulder but all hope would have been gone at that point. There would have been nothing left to do but tend the dying as long as he could and wait for the end.

How did Percy Fawcett face that end? If there had been any hope at all of getting out he would have kept going until he dropped in his tracks, so he must have been too weak and crippled to go on. His choices included the opium in the medical kit or his pistol, but neither of those seems to fit his character. It's much easier to imagine him sitting there in the shaded green gloom of his beloved jungle, making notes in his leather-bound journal until he couldn't control the pencil any more, then placing the book beside the tree he sat against and looking out through the towering trees. Trying, until exhaustion pulled his eyes closed for the last time, to catch a glimpse of the lost city he'd spent so many years searching for.

Bibliography

[i] Buckham, P.W. (1830); *The Theatre of the Greeks*
[ii] Grann, D. (2008); *The Lost City of Z*
[iii] *Stations of the British Army, 3 July 1886*
[iv] *Fawcett's Amazonia*
http://www.fawcettsamazonia.co.uk/program.htm
[v] Grann, D. (2008); *The Lost City of Z*
[vi] Royal Geographical Society; *Fawcett, Lt Col Henry Harrison – Administrative & Biographical History*
[vii] English Heritage; *History of Pendennis Castle*
http://www.english-heritage.org.uk/daysout/properties/pendennis-castle/history-and-research/history/
[viii] Galton, F. (1855); *The Art of Travel, or, Shifts and Contrivances Available in Wild Countries*
[ix] Royal Geographical Society; *Fawcett, Lt Col Henry Harrison – Administrative & Biographical History*
[x] Royal Geographical Society; *Fawcett, Lt Col Henry Harrison – Administrative & Biographical History*
[xi] Grann, D. (2008); *The Lost City of Z*
[xii] Janzen, D.H. (1974); *Tropical Blackwater rivers*
[xiii] *Percy Fawcett – The Lost Explorer*

http://bilgin.esme.org/Dreamland/Articles/PercyFawcettTheLastoftheGreatExplorers.aspx
[xiv] *Percy Fawcett – The Lost Explorer*

http://bilgin.esme.org/Dreamland/Articles/PercyFawcettTheLastoftheGreatExplorers.aspx
[xv] The Geographical Journal, Vol. XXXVII, Fawcett, P.H. (1911); *FURTHER EXPLORATIONS IN BOLIVIA: THE RIVER HEATH*
[xvi] The Geographical Journal, Vol. XXXVII, Fawcett, P.H. (1911); *FURTHER EXPLORATIONS IN BOLIVIA: THE RIVER HEATH*
[xvii] Grann, D. (2008); *The Lost City of Z*
[xviii] Holmes, R. (2005); *Tommy: The British Soldier on the Western Front*
[xix] Royal Anthroplogical Institute (1951); *Report on the human remains from Brazil*

CPSIA information can be obtained
at www.ICGtesting.com
Printed in the USA
LVOW08s0906300717
543149LV00027B/829/P